Gunnar Karlsson

A Brief History
of Iceland

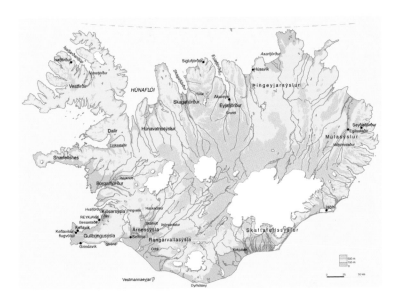

MÁL OG MENNING

A Brief History of Iceland
© Gunnar Karlsson 2000
English translation © Anna Yates 2000

Mál og menning
Reykjavík 2019

Cover: Emilía Ragnarsdóttir.
Map on cover by Niels Horrebow 1752,
  from Haraldur Sigurðsson: *Kortasaga
  Íslands frá lokum 16. aldar til 1848,*
  Reykjavík 1978.
Layout: Guðjón Ingi Hauksson
Maps: Jean-Pierre Biard
Printing: Prentmiðlun / Poland

1st edition 2000
2nd edition 2010
3rd edition 2019

ISBN 978-9979-3-4139-0

Mál og menning is an imprint
◊ of Forlagid
www.forlagid.is

Contents

1 Settlement

ICELAND REMAINED UNINHABITED FAR longer than most habitable places on earth. It was not until the Viking Age, which began around AD 800, that Norsemen began to build ships which could carry them out onto the North Atlantic with fair certainty of survival. Iceland's first historian, Ari Þorgilsson the Wise, says in *Íslendingabók* (the Book of Icelanders), written 200 years after the settlement, that the island was settled in a period of six decades, from about 870 to 930 AD. This is known in Iceland as the Age of Settlement. Ari mentions no specific dates; when the Icelanders celebrated the anniversary of the settlement in 1874 and again in 1974, this was based on a date given in a later historical work, *Landnámabók* (the Book of Settlements), by a less cautious historian than Ari.

Long before this, an island called Thule, where the sun shone all night in summer, was known in European geographical treatises; some of these accounts are consistent with Iceland. Medieval Icelandic sources also say that there were Irish monks living in Iceland when the Norsemen arrived.

Doubt has been cast upon the idea that a large island such as Iceland could have remained uninhabited for so long, and hypotheses have been put forward that people lived in Iceland long before the Norse settlement. Such theories have, however, recently encountered a setback. Archaeological research had revealed that many of the oldest sites in Iceland are close to a layer of volcanic ash that covers much of the island, known as the Settlement Layer. In 1995, traces of this same layer were found in ice cores from the Greenland Glacier, which can be dated within a year or two to AD 871. This date is astonishingly consistent with the evidence of Ari the Wise.

According to Ari and the Book of Settlements, the first permanent Norse settler in Iceland was Ingólfur Arnarson, who settled in Reykjavík, where Iceland's capital would grow up many centuries later. Ingólfur's wife was called Hallveig, and some Icelanders can trace their descent from these first two settlers. The Book of Settlements tells of several men who had found and explored Iceland before

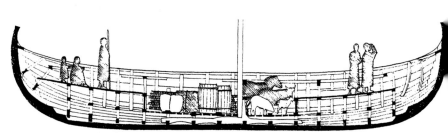

In 1957–62 the remains of five ships from the Viking Age were excavated at Roskilde Fjord in Denmark. One of them is believed to be a knörr, similar to those used on journeys to Iceland from Norway. The picture shows a longitudinal section of the knörr, with crew and goods, which could be bound for Iceland with settlers.

Ingólfur Arnarson, who was, according to the sources, the first permanent settler in Iceland, made his home in Reykjavík. Nine centuries later, the first urban community in Iceland grew up in the same place, and evolved into Iceland's capital. The choice of Reykjavík as capital is not known to have been linked in any way with its historical role.

Ingólfur, one of whom is supposed to have given Iceland its chilly name.

The Book of Settlements mentions over 400 settlers, and the places they settled around the country. Most were from the west coast of Norway, but many had lived for a while in Viking settlements in the British Isles. Some also came from other parts of Scandinavia, and a handful are said to be of Irish origin. The Norse settlers were accompanied by slaves, and perhaps wives, of Celtic origin; most of the settlers named were men, but not all. The

population of Iceland must therefore have been somewhat mixed, although the majority were of Norse origin, as witness their buildings and grave goods, and the language of medieval Iceland.

At the time of Iceland's settlement, Harald Fairhair was unifying Norway into a single kingdom, and according to the Book of Settlements many of the settlers were magnates who had fled the king's rule. The burial customs of the settlers, and other remnants of the settlement period indicate, however, that most of the settlers were ordinary farmers, who probably left Norway in search of farming land.

The origins of the first inhabitants of Iceland are demonstrated among other things by their grave goods. This brooch, from a burial mound in Breiðdalur, east Iceland, is of the Jalanger style, well-known from elsewhere in the Nordic world.

2 Old Commonwealth

IT IS AN ANCIENT CUSTOM FOR FREE males to assemble, in order to make important decisions. In the Viking Age this was customary all over Scandinavia, and assemblies were founded in all the Norse settlements around the North Atlantic.

The Icelanders established their assembly towards the end of the Age of Settlement, according to Ari the Wise. Later this was interpreted to mean 930 AD. The assembly, Alþingi, met at Þingvellir. The oldest Icelandic law code, *Grágás* (Grey Goose), provides information on Alþingi, as do many of the sagas.

Alþingi (parliament) was attended by *goðar* (chieftains with authority over a certain *goðorð* or group of farmers), who by law were to number 36, 39 or even 48. These chieftains could require every ninth farmer subject to their authority to attend the session. Farmers in the country numbered

4,500 (see chapter 5), this means that at least 500 men would attend parliament. In addition, parliamentary sessions were social occasions that attracted both men and women, and young people sometimes used the occasion to seek out a suitable spouse.

Parliamentary sessions were presided over by the *Lögsögumaður* (Lawspeaker), elected for a three-year term; one of his duties, in the days before written language, was to memorise and recite the laws of the land. At Alþingi, the chieftains sat in the Lögrétta (Law Council), the legisla-

Þingvellir. Almannagjá (Everyman's Gorge) lies across the picture from left to right. Lögberg (Law Rock) is believed to have been on the eastern edge of the gorge, slightly right of centre. On the plain below was the Lögrétta (Law Council). The Fifth Court assembled at Lögrétta, but the locations of the other courts are unknown.

tive body, each accompanied by two advisers. Chieftains also nominated farmers to man the courts, one for each of the four quarters of the country, and a Fifth Court to deal with cases that could not be resolved in regional courts.

In the regions, spring assemblies were held. According to a rule quoted in *Grágás*, three chieftains were to join together for a spring assembly; this meant that there were 13 spring assemblies in the country, three in each quarter, but four in the North Quarter, "because they could not agree on anything else," according to Ari. The spring assemblies were primarily judicial in nature; chieftains nominated farmers to judge cases arising within the district.

The chieftains also held *leiðarþing* ("road assemblies") on their return from parliament, in order to promulgate new laws and other innovations. The farmers under the authority of each chieftain were called his *þingmenn* (parliament men). By law, they had the right to transfer their allegiance to another chieftain, and the chieftain too could repudiate one of his followers. The right of the farmer to change allegiance is sometimes compared to the modern democratic right to vote. Some farmers are known to have used this right, but chieftains might also try to drive away local farmers they did not trust, and it could be risky to change allegiance. None of these democratic rights

The Lögrétta (Law Council) as imagined by Þóra Sigurðardóttir. Goðar (chieftains) sat on the central platform; each had advisers who sat in front of him and behind. In the centre stands the Lawspeaker, who presided over proceedings.

applied beyond the ranks of male farmers.

Iceland's government was weak, with the concomitant advantages and disadvantages. Chieftains aimed to maintain law and order among their liegemen. No king ruled the country, and no power existed to keep the peace, no army or police. In the 19th century this social system came to be known as *þjóðveldi*, the Icelandic word then used to denote a republic. Today *þjóðveldi*, which may be translated as Commonwealth, is used only for this decentralised social order that persisted in Iceland for more than three centuries.

3 Discoveries

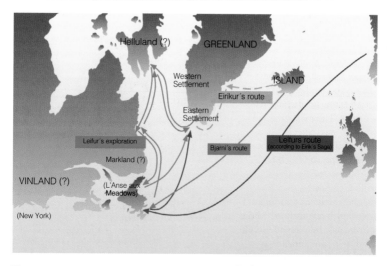

THE WESTWARD PROGRESS OF THE Norse in the Viking Age did not cease with Iceland. Before long they observed another land farther west, and in the late 10th century an Icelandic farmer in need of a place to go went exploring there. Born in Norway, he had killed people both in his home country and in Iceland, and been outlawed. His name was Eiríkur Þorvaldsson, known as Eiríkur (Erik) the Red. He discovered a mountainous coast with glaciers, sailed on around the southern tip, and finally found habitable land on the west coast. He settled in this land, which he called Greenland, with his wife, Þjóðhildur Jörundardóttir. Their son Leifur was probably born before they left Iceland. The settlement took place around AD 985 according to Ari the Wise. He does not mention the settlers being aware of any indigenous inhabitants, although they found signs of previous occupation.

People of Norse origin lived in

In Greenland the Norse lived in two separate communities on the west coast, Eystribyggð (Eastern Settlement) and Vestribyggð (Western Settlement).

Greenland for nearly five centuries. Ruins of 330 farms have been found, and the total population is estimated to have been around 3,000.

The discovery of yet more lands farther west is recounted in two different versions. According to one, Bjarni Herjólfsson, an Icelander, was carried off course when sailing from Iceland to Greenland, saw unknown lands in the west, but did not go ashore. Following his directions, Leifur ("Leif the Lucky"), son of Eiríkur the Red, went to explore these lands. According to the other saga, Leifur himself came across the unknown lands when travelling from Norway to Greenland in AD 1000.

The sagas are consistent in mentioning three lands; the northernmost was

Helluland (Slabland), the next Markland (Woodland), and the third Vínland (Wineland) where wild grapes and self-sown wheat grew. This land appeared to be an excellent place for settlement. The major attempt to settle was made by Þorfinnur Þórðarson, known as karlsefni, and his wife Guðríður Þorbjarnardóttir, with a company of several dozen people. Both of Icelandic origin, they made their expedition from Greenland. In Vínland Guðríður gave birth to a son, Snorri.

The settlers soon came into contact with indigenous people, called *skrælingjar* in the sagas: they were probably Native Americans, rather than Inuit. Initially relations were peaceful: the indigenous people traded skins for dairy products. Then conflict arose; the implication of the sagas is that the settlers provoked this. But the conflict led Þorfinnur and Guðríður to abandon their attempt to settle. This marked

The abandoned farm of Eiríksstaðir in Haukadalur in Dalasýsla, west Iceland, is traditionally believed to have been where Eiríkur the Red lived before he sailed for Greenland. Ruins of a Viking-Age longhouse have been unearthed there, presumably the birthplace of Leifur Eiríksson. The picture shows a recreation of the longhouse.

the end of the westward advance of Norsemen in the Viking Age, on the threshold of one of the most fertile expanses of land on earth.

In later centuries, doubt was sometimes cast upon the verity of the Norse discovery of America. These doubts were finally put to rest in the 1960s, when Norwegians Helge Ingstad and his wife Anne Stine discovered a Viking-Age site at L'Anse aux Meadows on Newfoundland. This is far too chilly a place for wild grapes, and it is now regarded as having been a staging-post on the route to Vínland, which must have been located farther south, perhaps in the vicinity of modern New York.

The construction technique of the buildings at L'Anse aux Meadows in Newfoundland clearly demonstrates that they were built by Norsemen. In addition, items were found on the site which were common in the Nordic countries in the Viking Age, but unknown to the aboriginal population of North America, such as a spindle whorl for spinning, iron nails and the brooch shown here.

4 Christianity

WHEN ICELAND WAS SETTLED, LITTLE Christian influence had reached Scandinavia. Iceland's first settlers worshipped the old Norse gods or *Æsir*: Óðinn and Þór, Freyr, Frigg and Freyja. In the 13th century Icelandic author Snorri Sturluson made a collection of Norse mythology in a book known as the *Prose Edda*. This is the most extensive source anywhere on the religion of the Germanic peoples in pre-Christian times, and also makes enjoyable reading, but it is hard to tell where true mythology gives way to the author's imagination. Little is known of heathen practices in Iceland, but the term *goði* (chieftain) is cognate with

This 7-cm bronze figure has long been believed to depict the Norse god Þór.

the word *goð* (god), and according to the sagas the chieftains originally held a religious office.

In the last decades of the 10th century, the first Christian missionaries came to Iceland; after a Christian Viking chief, Olaf Tryggvason, had seized power in Norway in 995, the mission began to bear fruit. A missionary sent by King Olaf baptised a chieftain from south Iceland, Gissur Teitsson the White, who was related to the king. Gissur and his son-in-law Hjalti Skeggjason undertook to induce the Icelanders to adopt Christianity. In 999 or 1000 they arrived in Iceland from Norway, accompanied by a foreign priest. Landing as the session of Alþingi was about to begin, they rode there directly.

At parliament, there were two factions, heathen and Christian, and it was foreseeable that Iceland would be split into two areas of jurisdiction by religious affiliation. Then the story goes that the Lawspeaker Þorgeir, chieftain of Ljósavatn, a heathen, undertook to make a compromise that both factions could accept. He went to his shelter, lay down beneath his cloak, and remained there until the following day, when he addressed the assembly, demanding a promise in advance that his compromise would be accepted. Then he proclaimed a law that everybody should take the Christian religion. It would, however, be permissible to worship the Norse gods discreetly, to eat horse meat, and expose children at birth. Then the whole company were baptised as Christians.

This is, admittedly, an unbelievable story, but it is the only one we have.

And it is clear that the Icelanders adopted Christianity without submitting to royal authority, whereas as a rule Christianity was forced on conquered peoples by victorious kings.

In the following century, the Icelanders founded a Christian church. Gissur the White's son, Ísleifur, trained for the priesthood in Germany, and in 1056 he was consecrated Bishop of Iceland, resident at his family estate, Skálholt in south Iceland. He was succeeded by his son, Gissur, who made Skálholt a permanent episcopal seat. In 1106, another bishopric was founded in the north, at Hólar. During the episcopate of Bishop Gissur (1082–1118), the tithe was introduced; this was a tax payable largely to the church, but also partly allocated to poor relief.

In Iceland, a system of privately run churches developed. Individual chieftains and farmers built churches, and donated property to them, sometimes the estates where they lived. They "managed" these properties as if they were their own, and passed them down

Crucifix from Ufsir in Svarfaðardalur, north Iceland. Carved of birch, it is believed to date from the first half of the 12th century.

to their sons. This system largely persisted throughout the Commonwealth period (Chapter 9), and is not entirely extinct even today.

At Flatatunga, Skagafjörður, in north Iceland, 11th-century wooden carvings have been preserved which are clearly influenced by Byzantine ecclesiastical art. Here we see a fragment of a Last Judgement, in which a fantastic creature is either swallowing a man, or perhaps vomiting up a man previously devoured, who is to face the Last Judgement. The carvings, which probably originate from the medieval cathedral at Hólar, are preserved in the National Museum of Iceland.

5 Medieval Society

It is impossible to make a reasonable estimate of the population of Iceland until the time of Bishop Gissur Ísleifsson around 1100. He had a census made of all self-supporting farmers in the country, and they numbered 4,560. On this basis, the total population has been estimated at 40 to 50 thousand. This indicates that Icelandic society was large, relative to its numbers in recent centuries. In 1100, the population of Norway cannot have been much more than seven times greater than that of Iceland, whereas today there are 15 times more people in Norway than Iceland.

All Icelanders lived on farms. No towns developed in Iceland in the Middle Ages. Fishing was carried out from coastal farms, and also from seasonal fishing stations when fish, especially cod, came inshore. Cereal crops were grown in Iceland in the Middle Ages, mainly in the south, but animal husbandry (cattle and sheep) was the mainstay. Both provided meat, and milk for cheese and *skyr* (milk curd), and the sheep's wool was woven into cloth which was Iceland's principal export commodity until the 14th century (Chapter 11). The Icelandic way of life is well illustrated by the units of value used: *alin vaðmáls* (an ell, about

Plan of Stöng, a farmhouse of the Old Commonwealth period. I: Entrance. II: Longhouse, where the inhabitants sat in the evening and slept at night. III: Stofa, a room used e.g. for women's work. IV: Pantry. V: Latrine. The Icelanders of the Old Commonwealth built large homes that required copious amounts of timber, as if they had not adapted to the fact that they had settled in a land with few trees. Some people have regarded it as unlikely that such large buildings were intended for no more than about ten people, as would be the case if there were about 5,000 farms and 50,000 inhabitants in the country.

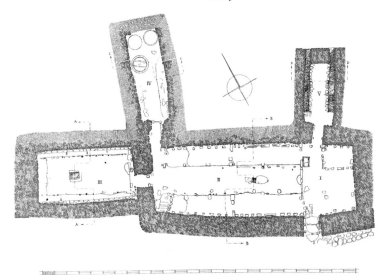

At Keldur in Rangárvellir, where Steinvör Sighvatsdóttir lived during the Sturlung Age, a longhouse has survived which is believed to be essentially from the Middle Ages, and hence to be the oldest building in Iceland. Turf houses are, admittedly, built by methods that require constant renewal, and so it can be difficult to ascertain the age of a specific building, but the form and location of the Keldur longhouse no doubt date from the Middle Ages. Thus Steinvör may be said to have walked through the doorway.

50 cm, of woollen cloth), *kúgildi* (the value of a cow), equivalent to 120 ells, and subsequently *fiskur* (fish), equivalent to half an ell.

The horse was mainly used for transport. (After the exemption that permitted the eating of horse meat, mentioned in the last chapter, was abolished in the 11th century, horses were no longer a source of food.) Carts were almost unknown, however, and Iceland had no roads, except for tracks gradually trodden by the hooves of horses, cattle and sheep. Horses were necessary, both to carry riders and as beasts of burden, and a good horse was always his master's pride and joy.

In the early years of Iceland's history, a clear division existed between the free and unfree. The number of slaves was perhaps never large, but both male and female slaves are often mentioned in the sagas. When their origin is specified, they are said to have been captured in Viking raids on the British Isles. Slavery was never abolished in Iceland, but slaves are not mentioned after contemporary sources become available in the 12th century.

Another clear division existed, between men and women. Women played no part in government. They could, admittedly, have authority over a group of farmers in a goðorð, but they had to appoint a man to perform their duties, and they were not nominated to serve in courts. The sagas, however, tell of various women whose personal qualities and character won them as much respect as any man. In the 13th century Steinvör Sighvatsdóttir, daughter of a chieftain, lived at Keldur in south Iceland. On one occasion she was nominated, along with the Bishop of Skálholt, to arbitrate in a dispute; if they could not agree, Steinvör alone was to arbitrate.

Yet another distinction appears as early as in the laws of the Commonwealth, which was to persist through Icelandic history. The ruling class wanted to divide Iceland into two kinds of people: farmers and their wives, and landless workers who were contracted by the year to work for farmers, and lived in their homes. Tireless efforts were made to prevent the development of two other social classes: casual workers who sold their labour to the highest bidder at any season, and householders who were resident by the sea, living by fishing, and had neither land nor livestock.

6 Sagas

Like other Christian nations of Europe in the Middle Ages, the Icelanders learned to read Latin script and used it to write books on vellum. But the Icelandic church was more worldly than other European churches; ecclesiastical culture was closer to the people's culture. Many chieftains became Christian priests, and more was written in the vernacular, Old Norse, and less in Latin than was the rule in Europe.

Perhaps this may be attributed to the fact that the leaders of Icelandic society were also priests of the heathen religion, who themselves decided to make the "white Christ" their god instead of Þór or Freyr. In addition to this, Iceland had no royal officials to enforce law and order in society. Thus the Icelanders became preoccupied with the question of how conflict could be restrained, but without condemning the individual's prerogative to defend his honour and that of his family by blood vengeance. Hence they had a perennial interest in stories of people who succeeded, or failed, at preserving the peace; material was gathered for story-telling, forming the basis for sagas written on vellum in the 13th and 14th centuries.

Icelandic saga-writing began with stories of the nation's origins, Ari the Wise's Book of Icelanders and the oldest version of the Book of Settlements, to which additions were made in later versions (Chapter 1). In the 12th century, Icelanders also began to write sagas of kings, especially kings of Norway, but also of Denmark. This literary form reached its zenith in the 13th century with Snorri Sturluson's Heimskringla (Orb of the World), a history of the kings of Norway.

The Sagas of Icelanders or family sagas began to be written in the late 12th or early 13th century. These are the most remarkable form of Old Icelandic literature, because the heroes of most of the stories are Icelandic farming folk. The events of the sagas take place largely in the period 930–1030; they recount, in highly realistic terms by the standards of medieval literature, tales of conflict and peace agreements, love and thwarted ambition. Written in prose form, the sagas employ a narrative technique reminiscent of the modern novel. Events are staged, characters speak

Möðruvallabók (the Möðruvellir Book) is the greatest of the manuscripts of Icelandic family sagas, containing 11 sagas on 189 leaves. The book is preserved at the Árni Magnússon Manuscript Institute in Reykjavík.

in direct speech, and their thoughts are implied by their external behaviour, rarely by direct description. The Sagas of Icelanders are the largest category of sagas, numbering about 40, in addition to short stories (þættir). No author of an Icelandic saga is identified by name, but scholars have attempted to find some of the authors among the chieftains of the 13th century.

Icelanders also wrote sagas of other kinds, which are regarded as less remarkable. Sagas of Bishops were written in some cases in order to support an application to the Holy See to acknowledge the sanctity of certain Icelandic bishops; yet these sagas survive almost exclusively in Old Norse, not in Latin. Secular contemporary sagas deal largely with events among Icelandic chieftains in the 12th and 13th centuries; most of these are preserved in the Sturlunga Saga compilation, which was put together in the early 14th century. Sagas of Ancient Times tell of kings and heroes in prehistoric Scandinavia, before the advent of the Norse kingdoms of the Viking Age. Icelanders also translated various European literature, such as hagiographies (lives of saints) and Sagas of Chivalry (prose translations of French courtly chansons de geste and other European literature), and wrote their own pastiches in the same style.

Icelandic vellum manuscripts often have beautiful illuminated capitals, and sometimes also illustrations in the margins. Here is a page of the largest of the manuscripts, Flateyjarbók (the Flatey Book). It contains 225 leaves, which would have required the hides of 113 calves. The content of the book is mainly sagas of kings. In the 17th century the Flatey Book was presented to the King of Denmark, and it was preserved in the Royal Library in Copenhagen until it was returned to Iceland in 1971. This was one of the first two books sent back to Iceland, when the Danes returned all the Icelandic manuscripts in their keeping whose content was defined as relevant to the Icelandic cultural heritage.

7 End of the Commonwealth

UNLIKE A MODERN MEMBER OF parliament, a chieftain could gain control of more than one goðorð. In the latter half of the 12th century, there was a growing tendency for more than one *goðorð* to belong to the same man. The sagas sometimes mention a *goðorð* being given to a man who already had one. Some people who inherited a goðorð appear not to have wanted it (any more than we all want to sit in parliament in modern times), while some proved incapable of providing their liegemen with the protection expected of them. This trend continued, until early in the 13th century the majority of the country had become concentrated in the hands of eight magnates. In addition, some of these were close relatives, so that five families or clans practically ruled the country.

At about the same time, conflict intensified. There were more battles, with more numerous forces, and they travelled longer distances to make war. This may have been partly a consequence of the concentration of power: the magnates could raise larger forces of farmers from among their followers, and they had to travel farther to the next magnate's territory.

Another contributory factor may have been the influence of the king of Norway. At this time, royal power was in the ascendant in Norway after a prolonged period of discord and civil war. In 1217 King Hakon Hakonson succeeded to the throne; he would reign, largely in peace, until 1263. The king appears to have resolved to gain control of all lands around the North Atlantic inhabited by Norse people.

This period of internal strife between magnates, and royal attempts to take control of Iceland, is known in Iceland as the Sturlung Age, in reference to one of the magnate clans. The precise dating of the Sturlung Age varies, but it is logical to date it from when the sources first mention plans by the Norwegian crown to take over Iceland, i.e. 1220. This was when an Icelandic chieftain of the Sturlung clan, Snorri Sturluson, left Norway for Iceland, having undertaken to win Iceland over to the king.

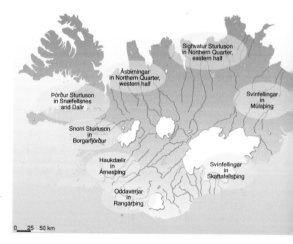

Dominions of the principal magnates in the first half of the 13th century. Eight magnates controlled the majority of the country, all of them from five major clans.

Jóhannes Geir's painting, Military Foray in Skagafjörður, may be a reference to the Örlygsstaðir battle of 1238, or another battle at Haugsnes in 1246, which cost about 100 lives.

Snorri, admittedly, never fulfilled this promise, and one source states that he did not try very hard. But 15 years later another member of the Sturlungs undertook the same task. This was Snorri's nephew, Sturla Sighvatsson. Sturla launched a campaign of attacks on other magnates, aiming to induce them to flee to Norway, where the king would force them to abdicate their powers. But Sturla's campaign came to an end at the Battle of Örlygsstaðir in north Iceland, on 21 August 1238. Sturla and his father, Sighvatur, led a force of several hundred, perhaps as many as 1,000, against nearly 1,700 men led by the magnate of the region, Kolbeinn Arnórsson the Young, and Gissur Þorvaldsson from the south, a descendant of Gissur the White (Chapter 4). Both Sturla and Sighvatur died in the battle, with about 50 of their supporters; their opponents lost only seven men.

In the following years the conflict continued; among those who died was the chieftain and literary genius Snorri Sturluson, in 1241. In 1258 the king sent Gissur, the victor of Örlygsstaðir, home to Iceland, with the title of jarl (earl) of Iceland. He succeeded in 1262 in inducing the chieftains and representatives of farmers in the north, the west and south Iceland to swear allegiance to the king and undertake to pay him taxes in the future. In the next two years the same undertaking was given for the East Fjords and south-eastern Iceland. Iceland had become a tributary land of the King of Norway.

8 Norwegian Rule

WHEN ICELAND BECAME A DOMIN-ION of Norway, Norway itself still comprised three or four jurisdictional regions, each with its own laws. In addition, other dominions were subject to the crown: the Orkneys and Shetland were an earldom of the king, and the Faroes had also been a tributary territory of the king since the 11th century. The Greenlanders submitted to royal authority before the Icelanders. King Hakon died in 1263 in the Orkneys, on a campaign to ensure royal authority over the Hebrides and the Isle of Man.

Hakon's son and successor Magnus, known as the Law-Reformer, abandoned his claim to the Hebrides and the Isle of Man. Instead he gave priority to consolidating the kingdom of Norway itself. He had the nation's laws revised twice, so that all parts of Norway were subject essentially to the same laws by the time he died in 1280.

The Icelanders also received two new law codes during Magnus' reign. In 1271 the king sent to Iceland a new legal code known as *Járnsíða* (Ironside), followed by another book which bears the name of its main author, Jón Einarsson, *Jónsbók* (Jón's Book). But, contrary to developments in Norway, this second revision led Iceland further from conformity with Norwegian law. *Jónsbók* was admittedly based largely on Norwegian law, but it was drawn up for Iceland alone, and it remained in force there for four to five centuries, while Norwegian law underwent many revisions. Jónsbók thus made Iceland a separate jurisdictional area under royal rule.

Iceland's system of government was radically altered by *Járnsíða* and *Jónsbók*. Alþingi continued to meet, but the Law Council, which had been a legislative body, became primarily a court of law. The four regional courts, the Fifth Court and the spring assemblies were abolished; new officials, *lögmenn* (lawmen) and *sýslumenn* (district commissioners) presided over regional court proceedings as required.

Iceland was also assigned its own administrative officials. Around the year 1300 a demand was first put forward at Alþingi that Icelanders of the old chieftain clans should be appointed royal representatives in Iceland. For centuries after this, most administrative offices were held by Icelanders. Only

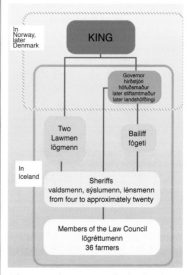

The system of government of Iceland under Norwegian and then Danish rule, until the late 17th century. Iceland had its own system of government, and the vast majority of its officials were Icelanders.

the office of governor (*hirðstjóri*), the supreme royal officer in Iceland, was held by foreigners as often as Icelanders.

Nor did Iceland become a part of Norway's system of national defence. No measures for defence of the country were taken, and it was only on rare occasions that the king attempted to induce the Icelanders to contribute forces or money for the defence of the kingdom, generally with little success.

Another factor which was to be crucial for Iceland's status in the long term was the development of the Nordic languages. During the period of the Old Commonwealth, the Icelanders regarded the dialects spoken in the Nordic countries as a single language, which they called Norse or Danish. But in the 14th and 15th centuries the other Nordic languages underwent considerable change, while the Icelanders' language remained almost unaltered. Thus the Icelanders stopped calling their language Norse, and started to call it Icelandic. Their linguistic isolation in turn served to help the Icelanders keep foreign law

A French book of coats of arms from about 1280 says that this is the crest of the "King of Iceland." The hypothesis has been proposed that it was the crest of Gissur Þorvaldsson, who was the first and only jarl (earl) of Iceland.

and foreign officials out of the country. Iceland thus retained a remarkable degree of autonomy within the realm.

In the 13th century Bergen became the capital of Iceland. The king lived in this splendid palace. It may have looked rather different then, as it was rebuilt in the 19th century.

9 Victory of the Church

THE WAY THAT SECULAR AND ecclesiastical power were intertwined in Iceland (Chapter 4) would probably be regarded today as beneficial for the church and religious life. But in the Middle Ages the church sought autonomy, and many church leaders wanted above all for the church of their country to comply with the European standards of the time.

In 1178 a bishop of a new breed came to the see of Skálholt: Þorlákur Þórhallsson, a monk, not kin to any magnates. He arrived with a mandate from the Archbishop of Trondheim, to claim authority over all those properties which had been "donated" to the church but which were treated as private enterprises. There was no dispute over ownership of the churches or their properties; the owners were the saints to whom the churches were dedicated. The dispute concerned who should manage the estates for them: descendants of the donor, or the bishop.

Bishop Þorlákur started by claiming authority over individual church estates in the east, with some success. But in the south he encountered intransigent opposition from Iceland's most powerful magnate, Jón Loftsson of Oddi. One may well suspect that the vendetta had a more personal aspect, as Þorlákur had been raised at Oddi, and his sister was Jón's concubine. In the end, the bishop had to back down, but his claim to authority over church properties was not forgotten by Icelandic clerics.

Other aspects of the campaign for church autonomy (*libertas ecclesiae*) were more successful. In 1190 the

In the Middle Ages, three Icelanders attained what was regarded as holy status. They were all bishops of Icelandic dioceses, and they are depicted on this altar frontal from the see of Hólar. Two were involved in the campaign for church autonomy: Bishop Þorlákur Þórhallsson of Skálholt, right, and Bishop Guðmundur Arason of Hólar, left. Between them is Jón Ögmundsson, the first bishop of Hólar. None of these home-grown saints was recognised by the Pope, until Þorlákur was canonised in 1985.

Archbishop sent out instructions that chieftains (those who held a goðorð) could no longer be ordained to the priesthood. This command appears to have been observed. Hence the tie that bound religious observance to secular government, perhaps a relic of heathen times, was broken.

In the first half of the 13th century, secular and ecclesiastical power came into conflict in the north of Iceland. For a period of decades, a large number of Iceland's chieftains came into conflict with Bishop Guðmundur Arason of Hólar. The dispute appears to have focussed principally on whether the bishop or the local chieftain, who had arranged Guðmundur's appointment to the episcopate, should have control of the resources of the see.

This dispute was never resolved, and after the death of Bishop Guðmundur in 1237 the Archbishop of Trondheim started sending foreign bishops to Iceland. Little is known of their efforts to promote ecclesiastical autonomy.

In 1269 Árni Þorláksson was appointed bishop of Skálholt, the first Icelandic bishop at the see for over three decades. He revived Þorlákur's claim for authority over church properties, and achieved rather more than half a victory. In 1297 Bishop Árni reached an agreement with King Erik Magnusson of Norway, whereby the bishop gained control of all properties entirely owned by the church, while properties in which the landowners retained a half-share or more would continue to be managed by them. The majority of Icelandic church properties became subject to the bishop's authority. This was a huge financial blow to the Icelandic chieftains. It became still more important to them to gain royal office and income.

This carved stone image was found in a churchyard at Síðumúli, Borgarfjörður. It was said to have been the gravestone of the murdered sweetheart of the farmer's daughter. It is, however, more likely that the statue stood in the church before the Reformation, and represents the Virgin Mary.

10 Collapse of the North Atlantic Realm

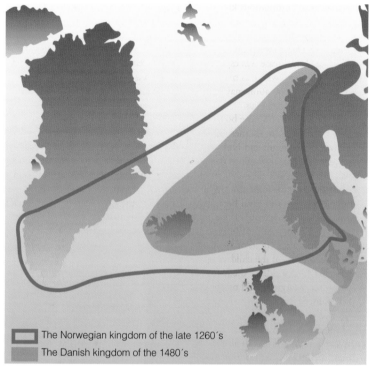

☐ The Norwegian kingdom of the late 1260's
■ The Danish kingdom of the 1480's

THE REALM OF THE KING OF NORWAY, when Iceland became a part of it, was centred on the North Atlantic. It stretched from the west coast of Greenland to the Barents Sea in the north, and south to Gothenburg and the Orkneys (since the Hebrides and Isle of Man can hardly be included, cf. Chapter 8). Purely in terms of distance, Iceland was not far from the middle of this domain; it was within a week's travel of the main centres, the royal court at Bergen and the archiepiscopal see at Trondheim. Just over two centuries later, the capital of the state was the city of Copenhagen on the Sound, and

The alteration of Iceland's position, from being part of the marine empire of the King of Norway to belonging to the territorial realm of the King of Denmark.

Iceland was at the westernmost point of the kingdom.

It was King Hakon (1299–1319), son of Magnus, who turned the thrust of the state to the south and east. He moved his court from Bergen to Oslo, and arranged a marriage between his daughter Ingeborg and the brother of the Swedish king, when she was one year old. Their son, Magnus, inherited the thrones of Sweden and Norway in 1319, at the age of three.

Norway as an autonomous kingdom had thus practically ceased to exist. The mid-14th century also saw the Black Death sweep through Scandinavia. The disease was especially virulent in Norway, where as many as two-third of the population may have died in successive epidemics.

In the period 1376–80 the boy king Olaf, son of Hakon, inherited the crowns of Denmark and Norway. Thus Iceland became subject to the Danish throne, a relationship that was not finally broken off until 1944. Olaf was also of the Swedish royal house (which ruled Finland too). It is easy to imagine the idea of a unified Nordic realm forming in the mind of Queen Margrethe, mother of the child king. But in 1387 Olaf suddenly died, aged 17. However, Margrethe did not give up her plans. She contrived to have herself elected regent in all the Nordic kingdoms, and to have her six-year-old foster-son nominated heir to all the thrones. In 1397 an attempt was made in the Swedish city of Kalmar to establish a permanent union of the states.

Throughout the existence of the Kalmar Union its kings sat in Denmark. The Swedes were sometimes parties to the Union, sometimes not, until they withdrew permanently in 1521. Norway was, however, ruled by the Danish king until 1814, when it was forced to submit to the Swedish crown, leaving Iceland, the Faroes and Greenland as Danish dominions.

By this time Greenland had once again become part of the Danish realm; medieval Denmark, which was far from being a naval power had "lost" Greenland for two centuries. The last known occasion when a ship arrived in Norway from Greenland was in 1410. When a search was eventually made for Nordic Greenlanders in the early 17th century, only Inuits were found.

In the 15th century the King of Denmark also gave up Shetland and the Orkneys. King Christian I had spent so freely to ensure his control of the duchies of Schleswig and Holstein that in 1468 he had to mortgage the islands to the King of Scotland in order to pay his daughter's dowry. The mortgage has never been redeemed.

A caricature from the time of Queen Margrethe, depicting her and King Albrecht of Sweden, whom she succeeded in having overthrown.

11 The Beginning of Stockfish Exports

ICELAND'S FIRST SETTLERS MUST
HAVE known how to fish at sea, and
undoubtedly tried fishing as soon as
they reached Iceland. The sagas often
mention fishing, but almost never fish
exports. It is not until around 1300
that fish exports are mentioned in reliable sources. Icelandic fish is first noted
in English import records in 1307.
In 1340 a court ruling was made in
Norway that merchants were obliged
to pay tithes on fish, fish oil and sulphur imported from Iceland, and not
only on woollen cloth, as had been
customary. The ruling states that this
is because until recently little fish has
been exported from Iceland, and a large
quantity of woollen cloth, but that now
fish and fish oil are exported from there
in quantity.

Exports require both supply and
demand. The demand was brought
about largely by the development of
cities in mainland Europe. Fish was
one of the foods that were permissible
during religious fasts,
and hence demand
for it grew as
the

urban population rose, and people
needed foods for the fast, but had no
easy access to grain. Until this time,
German merchants had been able to
buy ample Norwegian fish in Bergen,
but by 1300 Norwegian merchants
started importing Icelandic fish to sell
to the Germans.

The supply may also have increased
in Iceland as the Icelanders learned to
exploit the annual winter migrations of
cod close to the south and southwest
coast, where they spawn in shallow
waters. It was in the years after 1300
that seasonal fishing stations became
established on the southwest coast,
and the wealthiest sector of society
began to congregate in this region. The
most powerful chieftains had almost
all been based inland. Now the pros-
perous elite began to settle along the
coast between Selvogur in the southwest and Vatnsfjörður in the West
Fjords. Hvalfjörður and Hafnarfjörður
developed into Iceland's most important trading centres. The royal
administration in Iceland
was located at
Bessastaðir
(now

*During the winter fishing season, fishermen lived in small, low-roofed turf shacks, where they
slept two to a bed. This shack which has survived at Stokkseyri, south Iceland, is known as
Þuríðarbúð (Þuríður's Shack) after Þuríður Einarsdóttir, who for 25 years was helmswoman of
a boat that fished from Stokkseyri in the first half of the 19th century. It was not uncommon
for women to crew fishing boats, but they very rarely stood at the helm.*

the presidential residence). The Westman Islands came into royal hands, and yielded so much revenue that officials in Copenhagen, whose geographical knowledge of Danish dominions could be somewhat hazy, sometimes referred to the country as "Iceland and the Westman Islands."

This period saw the development of the mixed agrarian/fishing society that typified the Icelandic economy for centuries. In January or February, people travelled from rural areas to the fishing stations, where they remained until spring, fishing from small boats. This was the most favourable fishing season, as fish stocks were plentiful, the weather was cool enough to permit fish to be dried before spoiling, and relatively few hands were required on the farm.

People were thus domiciled in rural areas, on farms. Fishing villages that were inhabited all year did not begin to evolve until the 19th century. It is debatable whether this reflects the economic efficiency of seasonal fish-

Stockfish was tied into bundles for export. The boy is hammering the last fish into the bundle to tighten the cord. Picture from a 17th-century foreign map.

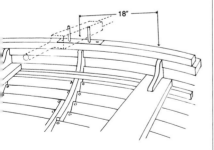

Fishing from open rowing boats may appear primitive, but in fact it required great skill in building boats, keeping them afloat in rough seas, and beaching them where there were no harbours.

ing, or whether people were prevented from settling permanently at the coast by various hindrances. Icelandic landowners, who probably had a large say in Icelandic legislation, did not regard the fishery as providing a reliable livelihood; this conviction may also have reflected their own wish to monopolise the workforce in rural employment.

The Icelanders fished largely using hand lines, and almost exclusively in open rowing boats, often equipped with a sail for use in favourable winds.

12 Plague

THE PLAGUE PANDEMIC KNOWN AS the Black Death that swept through Europe in the mid-14th century did not reach Iceland. But in Iceland, the 15th century began and ended with two plague epidemics which were probably no milder than the Black Death itself. The former epidemic lasted from 1402 to 1404, the latter 1494–95. Plague apparently never became endemic in Iceland, and no outbreak of the disease is known to have taken place after these two.

The period of the plague is the least documented of Icelandic history. No sagas were written about events in Iceland after a biography of a bishop who died in 1331. Only one contemporary annal, the New Annal, covers the period from 1393 to 1430. At this point it was abandoned, and no more annals were written until the 16th century. Sources on the epidemics are thus meagre, but the progress of the disease

may be traced in broad terms.

On the former occasion the plague arrived in Iceland at Hvalfjörður in the west, probably in August 1402. By Christmas it had reached the episcopal seat of Skálholt in the middle of the south, and Skagafjörður in the middle of the north. In 1403 the New Annal names people who have died, probably of the plague, from the West Fjords and as far as the middle of the east. The epidemic ravaged the whole country, and died out around Easter 1404, after 18–19 months.

The New Annal quotes various figures on mortality from the plague. Some are too high to be credible, while others are more moderate; these all indicate a mortality rate of over 50%. At the convent of Kirkjubæjarklaustur, for instance, the abbess and seven nuns died, while six nuns survived. By comparison, sources indicate a large number of abandoned farms about 40 years

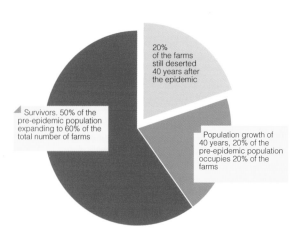

20% of the farms still deserted 40 years after the epidemic

Survivors. 50% of the pre-epidemic population expanding to 60% of the total number of farms

Population growth of 40 years, 20% of the pre-epidemic population occupies 20% of the farms

Estimate of loss of life in the earlier plague epidemic in Iceland, 1402–04, on the basis that 20% of farms were uninhabited when data next become available, about 40 years after the plague. About half the population are assumed to have died in the plague, while the survivors spread out to inhabit about 60% of farms. During the next 40 years the population rises by about 40%, which is about 20% of the pre-plague population. These additional people live on 20% of estates. This leaves 20% of estates uninhabited 40 years after the plague.

Deathbed scene from the 15th century. The woman's soul emerges from her mouth, to be received by angels. Demons wait at her bedside to take her soul if it does not fly upwards.

after the epidemic, when approximately 20% of farms remain uninhabited. From this figure it may be deduced that the mortality rate was at least 50%.

The latter epidemic, 1494–95, is described by an annalist, not at first hand, but based on the account of a man who had been 14 years old at the time:

„In this plague there was such loss of life, that noone could recall or had ever heard the like, for many farms were left deserted, and in most cases there was no-one left on the farms but two, or at most three people, sometimes children, usually two or at most three, sometimes yearlings, and some suckled their dead mothers. Of these I saw one, who was called Manga of Tungufell ... Where there had been nine siblings there were two or three left".

Mortality in this epidemic was probably rather lower than in the prior one, partly because it did not reach the West Fjords region.

It has long been maintained that the plague is carried by rats, and the fleas that live on them. Whatever the facts of the matter, the plague epidemics in Iceland cannot have been spread in this manner, as rats were unknown in Iceland until the 18th century. The plague in Iceland is thus an interesting example of a virulent outbreak in the absence of a rat population.

The effect of the plague was probably to sustain the status quo in Iceland. The drop in population would make more land available to the survivors, and hence reduce the motivation to settle by the sea and live by fishing.

13 The English Century and the German

In 1415 the lower house of the English parliament maintained that the English had been fishing off Iceland for six or seven years. Icelandic sources first mention English fishermen in 1412. An unfamiliar vessel was spotted off Dyrhólaey on the south coast; when the Icelanders rowed out to the ship, they found it to be English. Later in the century, up to 100 English vessels are believed to have sailed to Iceland yearly, and ten merchant ships on average sailed to Iceland each year to buy fish; these were mostly large vessels with a capacity of up to 400 tons and crews of up to 100 men.

Iceland was a land without defences, and the English could thus do more or less as they pleased. In 1425 they seized the governor of Iceland, a Dane, and transported him to England, where he wrote an indictment, claiming that the English had fortified their trading station on the Westman Islands, and even exterminated the population of some rural areas. We do not know how many of

The English had their headquarters on the Westman Islands. They fortified their trading post like a military installation, according to the Danish governor. This would of course be treasonous. The picture dates from the 19th century, but the moored ship is remarkably like the English merchant vessels of the 15th century.

his allegations are true, but one of the charges, that the English kidnapped Icelandic children, is confirmed by documentation. Icelanders were also said to give or sell their children to the English; this is the origin of Iceland's reputation among European geographers for centuries, as a place where people gave their children away to foreigners, but demanded a high price for their dogs.

In 1432 the Bishop of Skálholt, a Dane of high birth, was seized, tied up in a sack, and drowned. The deed was done by Icelanders, but some historians claim that the Bishop of Hólar, an Englishman, was behind it. But there is no doubt that the murder of the Icelandic governor Björn Þorleifsson in 1467 was the work of Englishmen.

The Danes made much of this killing, and the following year a five-year war began between England and Denmark. We Icelanders, on the periphery of European history, like to believe that it was Björn's murder that sparked off the war. Some also believe that the Icelandic fishing trade gave the English the experience they needed in ocean navigation that enabled them to start sailing regularly to North America in the following century, and to go on to colonise much of the world. In this light, Iceland's role in history is not so small.

But the English permitted themselves to be expelled from Iceland. In the latter half of the 15th century, Germans began sailing to Iceland, where they found themselves in conflict with the English. In the bloody confrontations that arose, the Danish crown generally sided with the Germans. By the mid-16th century, the English had been expelled from mainland Iceland, but they held on to the Westman Islands until 1558, when the crown seized all their assets there. After this the English had to settle for fishing in the waters off Iceland without going ashore, except surreptitiously.

At the same time as the English yielded, the crown turned on the Germans. In 1543 or 1544, all the 65 fishing boats owned by the Germans on the southwest peninsula were seized.

The English and Germans brought various new goods to Iceland. The Icelanders had never seen such variety of textiles and shoes, tools, weapons and wine. But the influence of these foreign nations would be eradicated by Danish influence over the coming centuries. A new age was dawning for many European nations, but Iceland was about to enter a period of unprecedented isolation as a remote Danish dominion.

In Iceland several English alabaster altarpieces have been preserved, and they are believed to have been brought to Iceland during the English Century. This altarpiece, from Hólar in north Iceland, depicts the Passion of Christ.

14 Reformation and Lutheran Culture

In 1536–37 King Christian III introduced Lutheranism into his realm by law, cut off relations with the Vatican in Rome, and made the church a state institution. Protestantism was at this

The cope of Bishop Jón Arason is preserved in the National Museum of Iceland. He has long been a respected figure in Icelandic history, largely because he was seen as an opponent of Danish royal authority. And from verses written by Bishop Jón, it would appear that he regarded the conflict over the Reformation primarily as a struggle between Danes and Icelanders.

time invariably strongest among urban dwellers, a non-existent social group in Iceland, and in Iceland there were no Protestants but a handful of young scholars at the see of Skálholt. The king also proceeded slowly in attempting to convert the Icelanders.

Royal representatives in Iceland, however, decided to exploit the king's abhorrence of monasteries, and in 1539

they seized the monastery on Viðey island offshore from Reykjavík. In the same year the royal treasurer rode east to Skálholt, probably intending to take possession of more religious houses. But at Skálholt they were ambushed by a group of armed farmers, who killed the treasurer and his followers. This wiped out the Danish government of Iceland, which was not replaced until a Danish naval vessel arrived in Iceland in the summer of 1541. By this time the bishop of Skálholt, Ögmundur Pálsson, had retired, having incautiously nominated as his successor Gissur Einarsson, one of the secret Lutheran sect at Skálholt. The Reformation was thus smoothly introduced there.

The title page of the Bible published by Bishop Guðbrandur Þorláksson of Hólar. Printed in 500 copies, it was sold at a price equivalent to two to three cows, depending upon the resources of the purchaser.

The bishop of the northern diocese, Jón Arason at Hólar, was left alone for the time being, and after the death of Bishop Gissur in 1548 he even started to intervene in the business of the Skálholt diocese. The king attempted to induce his Icelandic followers to arrest the bishop, but nothing was done until the autumn of 1550, when Bishop Jón risked travelling to the west of Iceland with only a small band of men and his two sons (in Iceland Catholic priests commonly lived with women and had children). They were captured, but no-one was prepared to keep them for the winter, as his captors feared that Bishop Jón's followers from the north would attempt to free them. Thus they were beheaded without benefit of law at Skálholt on 7 November. In Iceland this event is regarded as marking the end of the Middle Ages.

The fear of the men from the north proved well founded. At the beginning of 1551, 60 northerners rode south. They killed the royal treasurer and all other Danes they could lay hands on. Once again, the Danish royal government in Iceland had been annihilated. But government was reestablished the following summer, which saw the final adoption of the Reformation in Iceland, about 15 years later than in Denmark.

At the Reformation the monasteries were dissolved, and their possessions passed to the king. But the episcopal sees retained the bulk of their properties and revenues, and they became

The episcopal sees were the only places in Iceland with a concentration of population, until fishing villages began to develop. The picture shows Skálholt in the 18th century.

Iceland's principal cultural centres. At both sees were Latin schools which prepared prospective clergymen and others for further education in Copenhagen.

Guðbrandur Þorláksson (1571–1627) at Hólar had about 100 books published in the vernacular, which the Icelanders had previously called "Norse" but now called "Icelandic", including a translation of the Bible in 1584. Iceland differed from other Danish dominions in that the mother tongue of the inhabitants, and not Danish, became the language of the Lutheran church. As early as the days of Bishop Guðbrandur, the Icelanders began to see their language as a valuable national treasure. This conviction has been dominant in Iceland almost ever since, and hence modern Icelandic contains a very small proportion of foreign loan-words.

15 Monopoly Trade and Absolutism

THE 17TH AND 18TH CENTURIES MAY be called the Danish Age in Iceland; the power of the crown and Danish influence were on the increase.

In 1602 King Christian IV granted the merchants of three Danish cities exclusive rights to the Iceland trade. This marked the beginning of 185 years of monopoly in Iceland's foreign trade. The trade was confined to Danes, and prohibited all competition between traders.

The monopoly trade served the common interests of three parties. The crown prevented other nations from becoming interested in the country, and thus saved the potential expense of defending it, and the trade also generally yielded some lease revenues to the treasury. Danish traders made a considerable profit on the trade, which they used as a practice market in running a long-distance international trade without having to sustain competition. Finally, the monopoly trade helped Icelandic landowners retain their monopoly on the labour force (mentioned in Chapter 11), since the trade arrangement hindered the formation of urban centres of population in Iceland.

Absolute rule by the king was introduced in Denmark in 1661, by the crown in alliance with the bourgeoisie against the nobility. In Iceland there was neither bourgeoisie nor nobility; hence those who represented Iceland in swearing allegiance to the absolute monarch at Kópavogur in the summer of 1662 were clearly uncertain whether they were renouncing any rights. And the domestic government of the country was not altered by absolutism. Not until more than two decades later was it reorganised to conform more closely to the Danish system. A new office of governor (*stiftamtmaður*) was instituted, replacing the hirðstjóri. This office was initially a sinecure, allocated to the king's five-year-old illegitimate son. But from 1770 governors resided in Iceland, and governed it in practice. Under their authority were two or three *amtmenn*

For a time, Iceland was divided up into trading districts around certain ports. Each was leased to a certain merchant, and the inhabitants of the region were prohibited from trading outside their region. Many of these trading ports later grew into villages and towns, and still exist today. The large number of trading ports in the west demonstrates the importance of fish exports. It was in the west that most fish was caught, and so the economy could sustain more merchants.

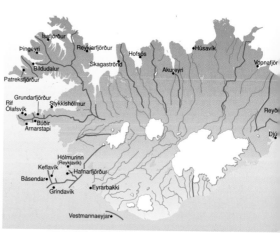

Danish rulers were resident at Bessastaðir (today the president's residence). The picture shows Bessastaðir around 1720. The building at the far right is a church. The tallest house next to it is the regional governor's residence, while at the far left is the treasurer's residence. Between them is accommodation for farm workers (rear) and sheds for livestock (in front).

(regional governors with responsibility for one quarter or half of the country), while finances were in the hands of the *landfógeti* or treasurer. The offices of lawmen and district commissioners, remained unchanged.

Absolutism gradually encroached on Icelandic life in the form of increased power in the hands of officials. The vast majority of officials were Icelanders (cf. Chapter 8), with the exception of the governor, treasurer and regional governors, some of whom were Icelandic, others Danes. The Icelandic officials probably had a considerable influence on Icelandic affairs, and tended to serve the interests of the landowners. But the Danish authorities gradually began to intervene more actively than before in the lives of the people. In the 18th century, for instance, measures were introduced to ensure that everybody learned to read.

The monopoly trade was abolished in 1787, but trade remained limited to subjects of the king of Denmark until 1855. While there was no legal hindrance to Icelanders trading in this period, business remained largely in Danish hands. Absolute rule proved

even more tenacious; it did not come to an end until Iceland was granted a constitution in 1874, as will be discussed in Chapter 19.

Representatives of the Icelanders accepted the King as absolute ruler of Iceland at Kópavogur (south of Reykjavík) in the summer of 1662. The event is commemorated by this monument.

16 Dark Ages

Icelandic history has long been presented as a romantic tale, with a time of early splendour until the end of the Old Commonwealth, followed by a long period of hardship, and culminating in a renaissance in the 19th and 20th centuries. Right or wrong, history has taught Icelanders that political autonomy means prosperity, while submission means decline. It remains a matter of debate how these lines of

witchhunts, which led 25 people to be burned at the stake in Iceland. And this was when Iceland suffered what is probably the only bloody invasion in its history: in 1627 a band of pirates from North Africa came to Iceland, abducted over 350 people and killed another 50 or so.

None of this is any worse than what was experienced in other European countries at the time. But the 18th cen-

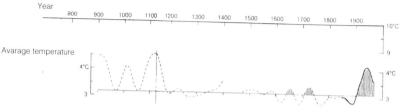

evolution are joined, as the fluctuations also coincide to some degree with climatic variations. It appears, in fact, that the climate is warmer when the nation is independent, but it would be difficult to produce scientific proof of such a causal link.

The 17th and 18th centuries have generally been viewed as the nadir of Icelandic life. The 17th century was the period of Lutheran orthodoxy, when fear of eternal damnation was the church's principal means of ensuring good behaviour. This was also the time of

Estimated average temperatures in Iceland from the 9th century until the 20th. Regular weather observations have been made at Stykkishólmur, west Iceland, since the mid-19th century. Prior to this period, temperatures are deduced from records of sea ice off Iceland.

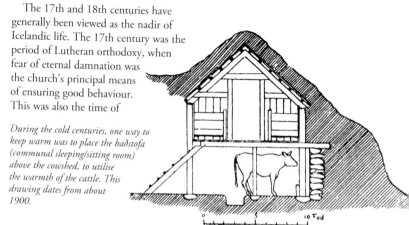

During the cold centuries, one way to keep warm was to place the baðstofa (communal sleeping/sitting room) above the cowshed, to utilise the warmth of the cattle. This drawing dates from about 1900.

The Skaftá Fires (eruption of Mt. Laki) produced an expanse of lava 580km² in area, or 0.5% of the area of Iceland. Much of this lava field is now overgrown with soft and yielding moss.

tury was a period of progress in much of Europe, not least in Denmark, while in Iceland it was a century of the greatest degradation. The clearest yardstick is found in population figures. In 1703 a census was made in Iceland, and the population was 50,358. In 1801 the population number had dropped over three thousand, to 47,240. This reduction was attributable to three blows suffered in Iceland.

The first was an epidemic of smallpox that struck in 1707–09. In mainland Europe smallpox was endemic as a childhood disease, costing few lives and bestowing lifelong immunity on adults. The disease only occasionally reached Iceland, infecting many adults, whose resistance was less. The 1707 outbreak, the first for 35 years, cost one quarter of the population their lives, bringing numbers down to 37,000.

The next blow was a famine in 1751–58, due to cold weather conditions, sea ice and poor fish catches. At this time the population fell again from nearly 49,000 to 43,000.

Two decades later the Icelanders had reached the 50,000 level once more, when the third blow fell. In the summer of 1783 a volcanic eruption began in Skaftafellssýsla in the southeast, sending lava flowing down the course of the Skaftá river, and hence known as the Skaftá Fires. The ash expelled by the volcano proved toxic to domestic animals, and it rose so high into the atmosphere that a haze covered the whole country – and in fact a much larger area. The following winter was exceptionally cold, which caused a famine. Harsh earthquakes in the south in the summer of 1784 destroyed about 400 farmsteads, and this made it even more difficult for people to gather supplies for the winter. These events led to total mortality from starvation and deficiency diseases of about 10,000, one fifth of the population. The Haze Famine was a huge shock to the Icelanders, who had begun to feel that they were on the road to progress, as will be recounted in the next chapter.

Birth of Reykjavík

At the session of Alþingi at Þingvellir in the summer of 1751, thirteen Icelanders formed a corporation to establish a factory-based woollen industry, and make other economic innovations in Iceland. The company was called in Danish *De nye Indretninger* (the New Enterprises), which became *Innréttingar* in 18th century Icelandic. The group was led by Skúli Magnússon, who had recently been appointed national treasurer, the first Icelander to fill the post. In Copenhagen he was promised a generous contribution from the state treasury, and use of the royal property of Reykjavík. Skúli decided to establish the *Innréttingar* workshops there. Thus the first homestead in Iceland, according to old sources (Chapter 1), became Iceland's first urban centre and later its capital. There is no evidence that Skúli had any such historical precedent in mind when he chose Reykjavík for the *Innréttingar*, and it would not have been in the spirit of the 18th century to do so.

Several squat wooden buildings were constructed in Reykjavík for wool-spinning, fulling, rope-making and tanning. These activities employed 60–100 people at their height. Two decked ves-

sels were purchased for fishing and to transport the goods abroad. Fourteen Danish and Norwegian farmers were brought in to teach the Icelanders arable farming. Sulphur, a vital ingredient of munitions at the time, was processed for export.

None of these businesses were successful. The king repeatedly contributed funds to the enterprise, until in 1764 the *Innréttingar* merged with a new company that was taking over the Icelandic trade. After this the *Innréttingar* were part of the Reykjavík merchant's business. The enterprise gradually declined, until it was abandoned in 1801–3.

Nonetheless, it was thanks to the *Innréttingar* that Reykjavík became Iceland's capital. When a decision was made to abolish monopoly trading in 1786, six trading centres were established in Iceland and granted privileges for economic development. The only one of the six that retained its status as a trading community without a break was Reykjavík, and 18 August 1786 is regarded as the foundation date of the city. After monopoly trading was abolished, competition was permitted between traders, and more than one

A row of single-storey wooden buildings were constructed for the Innréttingar along the path that led from the farmstead of Reykjavík to the sea. This path was later named Aðalstræti (Main Street). This house (no. 10) still stands there, the only one of the Innréttingar buildings which survives in near-original form.

Reykjavík 1836. By the Lake, which was somewhat larger at that time, stands the Cathedral, which still stands on Kirkjustræti. To its left, farther back so that the roof stands out against the sea, is another building which still stands. Built in 1765–70 as a prison, it later became the residence of the governor, and subsequently Government House, housing the government of independent Iceland. Today it is the Prime Minister's office. The building stands on Lækjargata; a large dormer has been added to the front of the building.

trader could be in business in the same community. Around the year 1800 Reykjavík had five shops.

Then the country's top administration moved to Reykjavík. After the Haze Famine and earthquakes of 1784 (Chapter 16), the episcopal seat at Skálholt was in ruins. The see was abolished, the assets sold, and the bishop and school transferred to Reykjavík. Around 1800, the same was done to the see of Hólar, and the responsibilities of the Hólar diocese were transferred to the bishop and school in Reykjavík. In 1800 the Alþingi was abolished to be superseded by a national High Court, a court of appeal between district administrators and the Supreme Court in Copenhagen. The High Court was founded in 1801.

The governor still sat at Bessastaðir, but in 1806 he opted to live in his own house in Reykjavík rather than at his official residence. From this time the office remained in Reykjavík, so that all the upper echelons of administration were located there. Iceland had gained an urban centre and a capital. This was one of Iceland's first steps into the modern world, though it was a small one; in 1801, Reykjavík was still no more than a village, with a population of 307.

Skúli Magnússon, "father of Reykjavík," is commemorated by this statue in a Reykjavík public garden.

18 Beginnings of Nationalism

As early as the middle Ages, the Icelanders were convinced that they were a separate people. At least from the 16th century, Icelanders could be found who were proud of their origins, and sensitive to derogatory remarks about Iceland in foreign publications. But all indications are that they were generally content to be part of the realm of Denmark. Until the 19th century the Icelanders were not a politically-conscious nation.

This may be deduced from an event that took place in Iceland in 1809. Denmark had become caught up in the Napoleonic Wars, on the side of France against Britain. The British domination of the North Atlantic meant that trading links between Denmark and

Poet Jónas Hallgrímsson.

Danish grammarian Rasmus Christian Rask maintained that Icelandic was in fact the old common tongue of the Norse, which had survived only in Iceland. He played an important role in promoting Icelandic self-respect.

Iceland were disrupted, and the British induced the authorities in Iceland to grant them trading privileges, in violation of the law (Chapter 15). When the governor forbade Icelanders to trade with a certain English merchant, he seized the governor, while his Danish interpreter, Jørgen Jørgensen, took over the government of the country. Jørgensen promised to make Iceland an independent democratic nation. The Icelanders made no attempt to defend Danish rule in Iceland, and most Icelandic officials remained in office during the reign of Jørgensen. But after two months a British naval officer arrived in Iceland, arrested the insurgents and took them back to England. With the same detachment as before, the Icelanders saw Danish absolute rule re-imposed in their country.

The same applied in 1814, when Norway ceased to be ruled by Denmark, gaining the benefits of one of Europe's most democratic governments under the Swedish crown, while

Iceland remained under the absolute authority of the king of Denmark. In Iceland no discontent was expressed with this arrangement.

It was not until after the July Revolution of 1830 in France that Icelanders began to exhibit any trace of political nationalism. The king of Denmark promised to establish four advisory assemblies in his realm. In the assembly to represent the Danish islands (Zealand, Fyn etc.), two seats were to be allocated to Iceland. Then an Icelandic student in Copenhagen, Baldvin Einarsson, proposed that the Icelandic Alþingi be re-established at Þingvellir as an advisory assembly for Iceland. This did not happen, and for a time the king nominated two representatives for Iceland at the Danish islanders' assembly at Roskilde.

In 1835 four Icelandic students in Copenhagen began to publish an annual, *Fjölnir*, which took up the proposal of re-establishing the Alþingi. One member of the *Fjölnir* group was poet Jónas Hallgrímsson, who imbued the Icelanders' nationalism with a new emotional content, inspired by the Romanticism of the time. He saw land and people as one whole, meant for each other for eternity. He wrote in a poem that Þingvellir had been created by God for the nation:

*Búinn er úr bálastorku
bergkastali frjálsri þjóð.*

(Built from lava by divine creation
A fortress for a liberated nation.)

The "lava fortress" of Þingvellir during an assembly of old, as imagined by the British artist W.G. Collingwood.

39

19 Jón Sigurðsson and the Independence Movement

IN 1840, KING CHRISTIAN VIII OF Denmark felt it was time to demonstrate his esteem for the small nation that had conserved the old language of the Nordic world, and also written on vellum the priceless sagas of ancient kings of Denmark. So the king proposed that the Alþingi be re-established as an advisory assembly for Iceland, preferably at Þingvellir. The new Alþingi first assembled in 1845, but in Reykjavík, not at Þingvellir. The founding of the new parliament was an important acknowledgement that Iceland enjoyed special status within the realm. The other Danish advisory assemblies represented areas with populations in the hundreds of thousands; Icelandic subjects numbered only 58,000.

At this time the Icelandic movement for independence acquired a leader, philologist Jón Sigurðsson, who lived in Copenhagen throughout his career.

When King Frederik VII suddenly abolished absolute rule in 1848, Jón Sigurðsson was ready with his theory that, according to the covenant agreed between the Icelanders and the king in 1262 (Chapter 7), authority over Iceland should revert to the Icelanders themselves, and not to any Danish authorities, when the king abolished absolute rule. Iceland was a domain of the king, not of Denmark. This amounted to a demand for autonomy; the king replied that no decision would be made on Iceland's status within the realm until the Icelanders had put their views at a special assembly in Iceland.

This assembly, the National Convention (*Þjóðfundurinn*), did not take place until 1851, in Reykjavík. By this time, the wave of liberal fervour that followed the February Revolution of 1848 in Paris had died down. And the Danes' high opinion of the people of the small saga isle in the north turned out to have its darker side: they were not willing to give up this little jewel in their crown. There was no possibility of agreement between the royal authorities and the elected representatives, who almost without exception followed Jón Sigurðsson's nationalist policy. The convention was adjourned before reaching any conclusion.

Two decades of wrangling over the governance of Iceland followed, from which a compromise gradually emerged. In 1871 the king assented to a law passed the previous year by

Painting of the end of the National Convention of 1851, by Gunnlaugur Blöndal. Though too young to have seen any of those who attended the convention, he had pictures of many of them. At the front are the representatives of opposing interests: at left is Governor Trampe, who adjourned the session in opposition to the representatives' wishes. To the right is Jón Sigurðsson, who protests against the adjournment.

the Danish parliament, on the status of Iceland within the Danish realm. Iceland was defined as an inalienable part of the Danish realm, but with special rights. An annual allocation of funds was also made from the Danish treasury to the Icelandic. This was partly in recognition of the fact that the crown had appropriated the property of episcopal sees and schools (Chapter 17), but the funding was mainly granted because it was necessary in order for Iceland to become financially separated from the Danish state.

The question of Icelandic autonomy remained unresolved. The Icelanders demanded a legislature and a minister in Iceland; the Danish government agreed to the legislature, but not the minister. A solution was reached in 1873, when Alþingi resolved to ask the king to give the Icelanders a constitution as a gift on the occasion of the millennium of the settlement of Iceland, the following year. This

allowed the Icelanders to back down gracefully. Alþingi became a legislative body, and one of the ministers of the Danish government would in future be Minister for Iceland.

The Icelanders held a national festival in 1874 to mark the millennium of the settlement of the country. King Christian IX visited Iceland on this occasion, the first king to visit the country. The king is depicted here holding the constitution he presented to the Icelanders. The statue stands in front of Government House in Reykjavík. The story is told of a little boy who thought the statue commemorated Iceland's greatest newspaper-seller.

20 Rural Society in Crisis

THE FORTY YEARS AFTER THE END OF the Napoleonic Wars in 1814 were a time of growth in the Icelandic economy. The number of cattle rose by a quarter, to over 27,000. The number of sheep doubled, to more than half a million. The fishing fleet grew by nearly 30%. At the same time the population rose by 35%, so that it was mainly in sheep farming that growth exceeded the increase in population. The expansion comprised mainly wethers, which produced, among other things, wool for export. Trade increased greatly among the rural population; grain imports rose by 60% per head, tobacco imports by 50%, liquor consumption per head rose sixfold, and coffee and sugar, previously almost unknown to ordinary people, began to be imported.

The increase in the sheep population was contingent mainly on the utilisation of wild pasture land. The possibility of using this land was mainly due to a period of mild climate in the 1840s and early 1850s. This growth and pros-

perity undoubtedly played their part in boosting the Icelanders' self-confidence, that led them to demand autonomy when absolute rule was abolished in Denmark (Chapter 19).

This all changed in the years between 1850 and 1860. A virulent outbreak of ovine scab reached Iceland, and spread through the sheep population of the south and west, leading to a 40% drop in numbers nationally. The warm period also came to an end, and the last four decades of the 19th century were probably one of the coldest times in Iceland's history. This meant that agriculture could support fewer people, and this was compounded by the fact that, due to the fluctuations in the population level that followed the Haze Famine, an unusually numerous generation reached marriageable age (around 30) at this time. The economic limitations imposed by the land thus became more tangible than before, and communities had to meet growing costs of supporting paupers.

Alþingi primarily represented farmers' interests; many farmers sat in parliament, and they constituted the overwhelming majority of the electorate. The initial response of parliamentarians was to tighten the restrictions placed by the old agrarian society on growth and innovation (Chapter 11). The king was requested to enact legislation against paupers marrying, in order

Sheep farming, with the emphasis on wethers for wool, meat and tallow, was the growth sector of agriculture in the 19th century. But it was based upon over-exploitation of the land and could not last indefinitely, especially not in cold periods.

A large farm in the 19th century. The church is built of wood, which had become common at this time. The gables of the farm buildings face forwards, which was a 19th-century innovation. Another innovation was the rectangular vegetable and potato garden in front of the farmhouse.

to prevent people from having more children than they could support. (At this point Alþingi was still an advisory assembly.) But the Danish authorities refused to pass any such legislation. Later, after parliament had acquired legislative powers, laws were enacted, and received royal assent, that placed stricter controls than ever before on the right to establish a home, without any animal husbandry, at the coast. The leaders of the farming class, Jón Sigurðsson's most loyal supporters in the nation's campaign for independence, thus showed little interest in the freedom of those who were below them on the social scale. On the other hand, restrictions on the economic freedom of workers were gradually

alleviated; by 1894, the obligation of workers to bind themselves by yearly contracts was in practice abolished.

The problems of rural society were of course not solved by restrictions, but by offering people ways out of their situation. These outlets were of two main kinds in the 19th century, emigration to America, and migration to fishing villages on the coast. These will be the subject of the next chapters.

Nothing upset Iceland's leading landowners so much as an increase in the number of paupers in society. English traveller J. Ross Browne made this drawing of the household at Laug, Biskupstungur, in 1862. There were seven children aged 6 to 16.

21 Emigration

A group of Icelanders setting off from a Canadian port bound for New Iceland. Drawing from a Canadian newspaper, 19th century.

THE WAVE OF EMIGRATION THAT took 50 million Europeans to America between 1815 and 1914 included about 15,000 Icelanders, if we count only those who never returned to Iceland. This was about 20% of the population, in the period of the greatest emigration. This is a much lower proportion than emigrated from Ireland and Norway, similar to Sweden, but much higher than the proportion of emigrants from Denmark and most other European countries.

The emigration wave reached Iceland rather late. Just after the mid-19th century a few Icelandic Mormons emigrated to Utah, and in the following years some individuals and small groups went to the USA. A group of about 30 emigrated to Brazil in 1873. That same year, mass emigration to north America began with the departure of just over 300 people from north Iceland. The peak of emigration was in the 1880s. In the six year period from 1883 to 1888, over five thousand people fled the worst ravages of the cold period that struck Iceland in the latter half of the 19th century (Chapter 20). With a little assistance from a measles epidemic in 1882, this emigration led to the last period of population decline in Iceland's history; in 1880 the Icelanders numbered 72,500, but in 1890 just under 71,000. Around 1890 climatic conditions began to improve again, and the Icelanders grew more optimistic about their prospects at home. In the 1890s emigration was much reduced, and it would not reach its previous levels again. In the period 1906–14, the number of registered emigrants only once exceeded 100 in one year. People were beginning to see potential in the mechanisation of the fishing industry, which will be discussed in Chapter 25.

Proportionally the greatest numbers of emigrants left from the north and east of Iceland. The eastern sector of this region had experienced especially large population growth in the good years in the mid-century and before (Chapter 20). In the 1880s, the harsh conditions had a greater impact in the north than elsewhere.

Emigration from Iceland had two unusual features. On the one hand, most of the emigrants went not to the USA but to Canada. At the time when emigration from Iceland began, the Canadian government was actively encouraging immigration, using agents who organised travel for the emigrants, and offered free farm land. The majority of the Icelandic emigrants intended to farm, so they found these offers tempting. In Manitoba, Canada, a tract of land on the west shore of Lake Winnipeg was set aside for Icelanders and called New Iceland. The Icelanders were to govern themselves, and could continue to use Icelandic as their official language. But the land was not good for farming, and before long the town of Winnipeg, far south of New Iceland, was the main Icelandic community in America. Considerable

Icelandic-language cultural activities persisted there for a long time, including the publication of two weekly newspapers and many books.

Another feature of Icelandic emigration was the high proportion of women. From other countries the vast majority of emigrants were male, but slightly more than half the emigrants from Iceland were women. This was partly due to the fact that women outnumbered men by an unusually large margin in Iceland (110.7 women per 100 men in 1870). A more important factor, however, is that Icelanders emigrated largely in families, and this may reflect the closeness of family ties in a rural society, and also that Icelandic women had few job opportunities in urban areas in their own country.

Log cabin in New Iceland, of the type built by the settlers – perhaps an original settler's cabin. The severe Canadian winters were a shock to many Icelandic immigrants.

22 Urban Development

In 1870 about two thousand people lived in Reykjavík, about 500 in Akureyri in the north, and a similar number in Ísafjörður in the West Fjords. Other urban centres were even smaller. Around 1890 only about nine thousand people, 13% of the population, lived in communities of 50 or more. In 1904 the number of urban dwellers had risen to 20 thousand, one-quarter of the population. The growth was sustained largely by two factors: increased trade, and the use of decked schooners for fishing.

In the first half of the 19th century, Iceland's foreign trade was confined to subjects of the king of Denmark, and largely in the hands of Danish businesses (Chapter 15). Domestic trade was mainly in the form of personal barter between farmers and those who lived by the fishery. In 1855 Free Trade was permitted to all nationalities. This led to little change until around 1870, when the British began to buy sheep on the hoof, to be slaughtered in Britain. These exports would prove conducive to Icelanders gaining control of foreign trade.

Prior to this, Icelandic farmers had started to form organisations to influence trade. Around 1870 they began attempts to take over trade, by founding large corporations and opening shops at trading centres. All these enterprises proved short-lived, except the oldest, *Gránufélagið*, founded and managed by pioneering entrepreneur Tryggvi Gunnarsson. But in practice this company soon reverted to ownership by its Danish creditors. In Suður-Þingeyjarsýsla a more cautious start was made. In 1882 a company was formed, called the Þingeyjarsýsla Purchasing Company (*Kaupfélag*

Farmers from Þingeyjarsýsla, north Iceland, visiting the market town in the early 1900s. At the far left is the oldest of the Cooperative buildings, constructed in 1883. Built onto it is another Cooperative building from 1902.

Þingeyinga), in order to deal collectively with the British sheep buyers. Before long the company was exporting sheep on its own account, and ordering British goods in return. The Þingeyjarsýsla farmers then noticed that, quite unwittingly, they had founded a cooperative. This purchasing company or cooperative was the first of a chain of cooperatives which became so firmly established that they survived the end of sheep exports around 1900. In the 20th century the Federation of Icelandic Cooperative Societies, together with its subsidiaries, grew to be the largest commercial enterprise in the Icelandic economy, until its collapse in the 1990s.

The business of Icelandic traders also increased many times over in the last third of the 19th century. By 1904 most of the foreign trade was in Icelandic hands, and it was three times greater than in 1870.

The expansion of trade was largely due to growth in the fisheries, which in turn was largely due to the fact that the Icelanders now started to fish using schooners, which could stay at sea for days or even weeks at a time, and which followed the seasonal migrations of fish around Iceland's

Schooners at anchor off Reykjavík around 1900. Such large ships could not dock at Reykjavík until the harbour was constructed in 1913–17.

coasts. In the mid-19th century about 20 schooners operated from Iceland. In 1904 they numbered 160, some of them up to 90 tons. They were, however, far from superseding the old open rowing boats, which still caught one-third more fish than the schooners.

Decked schooners were not a technical advance as such. They were similar to the ships that the English had used to fish in Icelandic waters as long ago as the 15th century (Chapter 13). The fishing gear was also primitive, largely hand lines. But the advent of schooners heralded new times in the sense that this was the first time that employment was provided by large urban-based private enterprises. Merchant Ásgeir Ásgeirsson of Ísafjörður, for instance, owned up to 16 schooners, with 220 crew members. The schooner fishery was thus the first stage of capitalism in Iceland.

23 Home Rule and Independence

UNDER THE TERMS OF THE constitution of 1874, the Icelanders had their own legislative assembly, while one of the Danish government ministers served as Minister for Iceland (Chapter 19). The minister's role was not only to be the executive branch of government; it was also in his power to decide whether legislation received the royal assent. The Supreme Court in Denmark also served as the highest court of appeal for Iceland.

In 1885 Alþingi passed a bill on a new constitution, proposing that Iceland should have a viceroy resident in Iceland, and a government of up to three ministers. This bill was, predictably, refused royal assent, and for the next two decades revision of the constitution was the main concern of Icelandic politics. These were years of conservative government in Denmark, and Iceland's demands were rejected out of hand.

In 1897 Valtýr Guðmundsson, an Icelandic parliamentarian resident in Copenhagen, offered to Alþingi an informal proposal from the Danish Minister for Iceland, that a minister

for Iceland would be appointed in Copenhagen, without other ministerial responsibilities in the Danish government, who would presumably be an Icelander. Valtýr argued in favour of a minister who would have the time and interest to promote practical progress in Iceland. This would make it easier to gain greater autonomy in due course.

Parliament was divided into two more-or-less equal factions, for and against Valtýr. In 1901 his proposal was finally passed by a narrow majority. But just at this time, the conservative government of Denmark fell, to be replaced by a liberal administration, which offered the Icelanders a minister in Iceland, and on 1 February 1904, a government was established there, with a single minister. This was Hannes Hafstein, poet and leader of the Home Rule Party (*Heimastjórnarflokkur*). At this time, parliamentary government was introduced: it was recognised that the minister required the backing of a majority of parliament. Home Rule entailed that all legislative and executive power in Icelandic affairs was contingent upon parliamentary authority.

The self-esteem of Alþingi as a legislative body after 1874 may be deduced from the fact that it had Parliament House built, for the equivalent of one-third of the normal annual expenditure of the Treasury. The building stands on Kirkjustræti and Austurvöllur in Reykjavík, and still houses Iceland's parliament. To the left is the Cathedral, originally built in the late 18th century, to which an upper storey was added in the 19th century.

Iceland becomes an autonomous nation; ceremony at Government House in Reykjavík, 1 December 1918. The Danish soldiers at the bottom of the picture are performing their last official duty in Iceland, as Iceland became a neutral country without military forces at independence. The flag which flies over the building had been acknowledged for use within Iceland in 1915, but was now Iceland's national flag.

The time seemed ripe for making an agreement with Denmark on the relations between the two countries, superseding the Status Act of 1871. Agreement was reached by a Danish-Icelandic negotiating committee in 1908, but opponents of this agreement, who wanted more autonomy, won a majority in parliament, rejected the agreement, and formed a new majority party called the Independence Party (*Sjálfstæðisflokkur*).

The following years were spent on complex debate on the relationship of Iceland and Denmark. But after World War I, 1914–18, national self-determination was the watchword of European politics, and the Danes themselves aimed to reclaim the Danish-speaking part of Schleswig from the defeated Germans. This led them to agree in 1918 to Iceland becoming an independent state, sharing a king and foreign policy with Denmark. It was declared that Iceland would maintain neutrality in all conflicts between nations, and would maintain no military forces. The Danish Supreme Court would remain Iceland's highest appeals court until the Icelanders decided otherwise; and Iceland's own Supreme Court was in fact established in 1920.

Hannes Hafstein, poet and Iceland's first government minister, was renowned for his handsome looks.

24 Women's Rights

IN THE MID-19TH CENTURY, WOMEN had as few rights in Iceland as elsewhere in Europe, but they gained formal equality under the law largely during the period 1850–1923.

For the first 20–30 years, it was mostly males, not particularly identified with liberalism or innovation, who sought to improve individual aspects of women's rights. In 1847, the Danish government asked Alþingi, as was then customary, which new Danish legisla-

Bríet Bjarnhéðinsdóttir made her first public appearance as an advocate of women when she gave a lecture on discrimination between the sexes in Reykjavík in 1887. Two decades later, she founded the Icelandic Women's Rights Association, and became its leader. Today she, more than any other person, symbolises the women's rights movement in Iceland.

tion it wished to be enacted in Iceland. These included a new Inheritance Act that upheld the old tradition that males had a right to twice the inheritance of women, although parents now could opt to allow equal inheritance rights to their daughters and sons. Alþingi unanimously requested the king to introduce these laws for Iceland, with the amendment that women would always enjoy equal inheritance rights with men.

The first step towards suffrage for Icelandic women was also initiated by a rural member of Alþingi. In 1882, women who were heads of households were granted the right to vote in local elections, by legislation passed in parliament the previous year.

During the next stage, in the last two decades of the 19th century, the lead was taken by males who were under liberal, socially-radical influence from Europe. Petitions circulated which demanded votes for women; nonetheless, the national rights of a male-dominated society were the focus of these years. Parliamentary bills on amendments to the constitution never went further than to state that women could be granted the vote by a simple Act of parliament.

Women first gained real rights after they began to campaign on their own behalf. In 1894 the Icelandic Association of Women was founded in Reykjavík. Its original objective was to ensure that women would have the right to study at the university to be founded in Iceland. The association had, however, ceased all political activity by 1906, when Bríet Bjarnhéðinsdóttir, editor of

Icelandic women have generally regarded their greatest victory in the campaign for women's rights as being the granting of the vote in parliamentary elections on June 19, 1915. The event was celebrated on 7 July that summer, the day that the Alþingi next assembled. The photograph is taken on Austurvöllur in front of Parliament House.

the Women's Paper (*Kvennablaðið*), was invited to attend a meeting of the International Woman Suffrage Association in Copenhagen. The following year Bríet founded an affiliated organisation in Iceland, the Icelandic Women's Rights Association, which still exists. Bríet led the association for two decades. Since then she has been remembered as a symbol of that campaign.

In 1907–09 the franchise in local elections was extended to married women, and in 1908 a Women's List in Reykjavík municipal elections won 22% of the vote and four of fifteen council seats. In 1911 Alþingi passed legislation on equality for men and women at all educational institutions, and on eligibility for all offices. Women gained the right to vote in parliamentary elections by a constitutional amendment in 1915, although voting rights were confined to those aged 40 and over. This age limit was to be lowered by one year per year, but

in fact it was abolished in 1920. While political rights had been extended step by step, laws on women's personal rights had also been amended, and in 1923 legislation provided for equality of married couples in the disposal of their property.

The first woman to take a seat in parliament, in 1922, was Ingibjörg H. Bjarnason, headmistress of the Reykjavík School for Women.

25 Industrial Revolution in the Fisheries

In 1902 a two-horsepower paraf-
fin motor was installed in a six-oared
vessel, *Stanley*, at Ísafjörður. The
motor was purchased from Denmark;
a sixteen-year-old boy brought it to
Iceland, installed it, and taught skipper
Árni Gíslason to use it. This marked
the beginning of mechanisation in the
fisheries, which was to revolutionise
Icelandic society in the first three decades of the 20th century, in a manner
similar to the industrial revolutions of
other European countries. When the
motor was installed in the *Stanley*, two
thousand rowing boats were fishing
off the coast of Iceland. By 1930,
there were still 170 of these, while
motor-powered vessels numbered over
a thousand.

Iceland had first made the acquaint-
ance of trawlers, large steam-powered
fishing vessels that fished using trawl-
nets, around 1890 when British vessels
started trawling in Icelandic fishing
grounds. In 1899 the first attempt was
made to operate a trawler from Iceland.
But successful trawler fishing began
in 1905 when a group of Icelanders

*The six-oared boat Stanley, fitted with an
engine, heralded the beginning of mechanisation
in the fisheries, and hence the Icelandic
industrial revolution, in 1902.*

purchased a second-hand trawler, *Coot*,
from Scotland, and operated it from
Hafnarfjörður. When the *Coot* ran
aground three years later, other people
had already jumped on the bandwagon.
In 1907 the *Alliance* trawler company
had a new trawler, *Jón forseti* (President
Jón, courtesy title of the late Jón
Sigurðsson), built in Britain. In 1912
the number of trawlers rose from ten

*The Scottish trawler Coot, the first trawler owned by Icelanders, began fishing in 1905. The Coot
had a twelve-man crew, all Icelanders except for two foreign engineers during the first year.*

to twenty, and their catches exceeded 20% of total fish catches. Before the Depression struck Iceland in 1930, the number of trawlers had reached 41. Then the last of the schooners had disappeared from the registry of shipping.

During the first three decades of the 20th century, the Icelanders' fish catches rose fivefold, while the number of people employed in the fisheries increased only by 50%. The bulk of the catch consisted of cod, which was mostly salted for export. Some years, quantities of herring were also salted in barrels, and rendered into oil and fishmeal.

The revolution in the fisheries may be attributed to some degree to the influx of foreign credit. The National Bank of Iceland (*Landsbanki Íslands*), owned by the national treasury, had operated since 1886, but it lacked funds to back much innovation. In 1904 a new bank, the Bank of Iceland (*Íslandsbanki*) was founded, largely owned by Danish shareholders. The bank lent trawler buyers up to half the purchase price of vessels.

The revolution in the Icelandic fisheries could not, in any case, have taken place much earlier than it did, as it was based on technical advances. The trawl net was not in common use anywhere until about 1880. The internal combustion engine, was nowhere used in fishing vessels until around 1900.

The expansion of the fisheries led to the transformation of society as a whole. Telegraph communications with other countries were established in 1906. Compulsory elementary schooling was introduced in 1907. A university was founded in Reykjavík in 1911. Shortly after 1920, the urban population was larger than the rural. The population of Reykjavík was at this time about 20 thousand. After 1915, the town had been built up with concrete buildings standing by straight, planned streets, with sidewalks concealing water and drainage pipes. Electricity, from hydro-plants, was supplied to buildings in the larger urban centres.

The trawlers brought unprecedented wealth. Their captains built themselves houses such as those shown here at right and left. Between them is the home of a schooner captain.

26 Beginnings of the Union Movement

ONE OF THE CONSEQUENCES OF THE economic revolution was the evolution of an organised union movement. In the last decades of the 19th century, skilled workers in Reykjavík had on several occasions attempted to found unions, but the continuous history of union activity in Iceland begins in 1894, when schooner owners in the Reykjavík area formed an association to attempt to cut the wages of sailors, who responded by forming their own organisation, *Báran* (The Wave). Skippers undertook to mediate, and the first wage agreements in Iceland were made. In the following years more *Báran* chapters were founded in other communities.

In 1906 a new movement arose among trade-unionists in Reykjavík, with the foundation of the labourers' union *Dagsbrún* (Daybreak). For decades a leading force in the Icelandic union movement, it later merged with other unions. In 1906–07 the number of unions rose rapidly. This was followed by a backlash of several years' duration, undoubtedly partly due to the fact that Iceland's campaign for independence was very heated at this time (Chapter 23), and most Icelanders wanted to perceive the nation as a united whole against the Danes. It was thus highly favourable for the development of the union movement when in 1913 a Danish contractor employed on the construction of Reykjavík Harbour refused to pay his workers according to the rates agreed by *Dagsbrún* and employers. The workers went on a two-month strike, which ended in victory for them.

Women were not included in the first unions, but in 1914 a women workers' union was founded in Reykjavík. Called *Framsókn* (Progress), the union continued to exist until it merged with Dagsbrún. In 1915 the Reykjavík Sailors' Union (*Hásetafélag Reykjavíkur*) was founded. The union maintained a two-week strike of the trawler fleet the following year. The same year, on 12 March 1916, seven unions founded a national federation, the Icelandic Federation of Labour (*Alþýðusamband Íslands*), which still represents the union movement as a whole on the general labour market.

Employers did not establish a formal federation until 1934, when they formed the Confederation of Icelandic Employers

In this house in Seyðisfjörður, east Iceland, a labourers' union was founded in 1897, perhaps the first association of unskilled land-based workers in Iceland. But it did not last for long.

The Reykjavík labour unions held their first protest march on 1 May 1923.

(*Vinnuveitendasamband Íslands*, now *Samtök atvinnulífsins*). Long before this, however, employers were negotiating jointly with workers, and in 1925 the legislature acknowledged labour disputes de facto by passing legislation on mediation.

Comprehensive legislation on unions and labour disputes was enacted in 1938. This legalised labour disputes, and formally acknowledged the union movement as a participant in the system of government. At this point, almost all Icelandic workers were unionised.

Employees of national and local government have also formed their own employees' associations.

Jónína Jónatansdóttir was the first leader of the Framsókn women workers' union in Reykjavík, 1914–34, and the first woman to serve on the executive committee of the Federation of Labour.

27 A New Politicial Party System

The Home Rule period, 1904-18 (Chapter 23), saw the development of two political parties whose principal difference concerned the means of wresting more power over Iceland from the Danes. After the treaty of 1918 this party division was obsolete, while parties based on class lines gained support. The Federation of Labour (*Alþýðusamband Íslands*), founded in 1916, also functioned as a political party, under the name of Labour Party (*Alþýðuflokkur*).

The next party was formed by representatives of the farming class at Alþingi at the end of 1916 under the name of Progressive Party (*Framsóknarflokkur*). In addition to being an agrarian party that backed the cooperative movement, the party was intended to be a liberal central party, similar to the British Liberal Party or Venstre in Denmark.

In the following years the old parties of the Home Rule era evolved into a right-wing urban party, which also enjoyed considerable rural support. In 1929 this process was completed with the founding of a new Independence Party (*Sjálfstæðisflokkur*), which has been the largest party ever since, except 2009-13, and draws support from all social classes.

The strong position of the party was partly due to the fact that it was the offspring of the two older parties, but also because the left lacked a clearly leading party. In the 1920s, social democrats and communists coexisted uneasily within the Labour Party; this ended with the foundation of the Icelandic Communist Party (*Kommúnistaflokkur*) in 1930. This rift between workers' parties was naturally perceived as undermining the labour movement during the Depression of the 1930s. Hence an attempt was made to unite the parties. This, admittedly, did not happen but the Communist Party merged with a splinter group of Labour, forming the Socialist Party (*Sósíalistaflokkur*) in 1938. And at the next election, the Socialist Party had more support than the Labour Party. Shortly after this, formal ties between the Labour

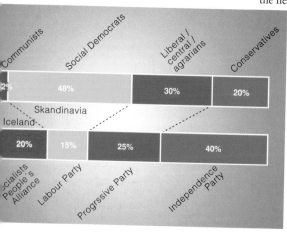

The Icelandic party system, c.1942–95, in comparison with those in Scandinavia, especially Denmark and Norway. The proportional support of parties has, naturally, varied more than is indicated here. In Denmark and Norway, the diagram is based upon election results 1936–39.

Jónas Jónsson of Hrifla was one of Iceland's most influential politicians in the first half of the 20th century. He was active in the founding of the Labour and Progressive Parties. He later led the latter party, and was a controversial minister of justice and of education in 1927–32.

Party and the Federation of Labour were abolished.

The Socialist Party, which loyally followed the Soviet line, found itself in a difficult situation during the Cold War period. Then the Labour Party was unfortunate enough to split once again, losing some of its members to collaboration with the Socialists. They campaigned jointly for election under the People's Alliance (*Alþýðubandalag*) name, and founded a party of the same name in 1968. In 2000, the Labour Party, the People's Alliance and the Women's Alliance (Chapter 32), merged into a new party, the Social

Democratic Alliance (*Samfylkingin*). But at the same time, a new left-wing party has emerged, the Left-Green Movement (*Vinstrihreyfingin – grænt framboð*), so the left was hardly closer to unity than before.

Support for the parties was for decades remarkably stable. The Independence Party generally had about 40% of the vote, the Progressive Party about 25%, the Labour Party around 15%, and the Socialist Party/People's Alliance 15– 20%. In the 1930s the Progressive Party was invariably the largest party in parliament, as it had the strongest support in rural areas, which were proportionately over-represented. After that, the Independence Party took the lead, although with some interruptions, as will be related in Chapter 29.

The Independence Party had much support from seamen and labourers. In this sense it resembles the British Conservative Party. The picture is taken on Seamen's Day in 1938. Ólafur Thors, leader of the Independence Party, speaks.

28 War, Occupation and the Republic

WHEN WORLD WAR II BROKE OUT IN September 1939, the Icelanders placed their confidence in their neutrality and remote location to keep them out of the hostilities. Even after Germany had occupied Denmark in April 1940, Iceland rejected British offers of military defence.

At this point the British felt the time had come to stop taking protestations of neutrality seriously. A month after the occupation of Denmark, on 10 May, British naval forces arrived to occupy the country. There was no resistance, and no doubt more than 90% of the nation were relieved that the occupying forces were British and not German.

In 1941 the British organised an agreement between Iceland and the USA, that the Americans would take over the defence of Iceland. US forces arrived in Iceland on 7 July 1941. This was before the USA had formally entered the war, and was the clearest example of American violation of its nominal neutrality at the time.

British forces in Iceland numbered about 25,000, American forces about 60,000. Both undertook bigger construction projects than had hitherto been known in Iceland. Airfields were built, for instance, in Reykjavík by the British, and by the Americans near the fishing village of Keflavík. The military had to employ many Icelanders on these projects, and the unemployment which had been a constant problem since 1930, gave way to a labour shortage. At the same time, due to war-related demand, prices rose enormously, both on imported goods and on the fish that the Icelanders exported. This led to a period of expansion with high inflation rates (up to 30% annually), and a higher standard of living than Iceland had ever experienced.

Sandbag fortifications at Lækjargata in downtown Reykjavík.

When Denmark was occupied in 1940, Alþingi passed a resolution that the king could no longer rule Iceland, and allocated royal powers to the government. A year later a viceroy was elected to fulfil the king's functions. Sveinn Björnsson, Iceland's emissary in Copenhagen, was elected to the office.

The terms of the 1918 treaty (Chapter 23) provided that it could be abrogated by either Denmark or Iceland, so that it would expire at the end of 1943. At this point the majority of Icelandic politicians felt that ties with Denmark should be broken off at once, in 1942, since the Danes were no longer able to uphold their part of the treaty. Others felt it would be dishonourable to cut the tie with Denmark while the Danes were under foreign occupation. The USA and Britain were also opposed to the idea, as they feared that the German propaganda would accuse them of inciting the Icelanders to repudiate their treaty with the Danes. Hence a decision was made to abrogate the treaty, and to found a republic in Iceland after the end of 1943, regardless of Denmark's situation at that time.

In May 1944 the abrogation of the treaty was confirmed by a plebiscite, in which 98.6% of the electorate voted, and a mere 377 people, 0.5%, voted against. On the birthday of Jón Sigurðsson, 17 June, the Republic of Iceland was founded at a ceremony at Þingvellir, attended by one-fifth of the Icelandic population in a mem-

Celebrations of the founding of the modern Republic at Þingvellir, 17 June 1944. Beneath the coat of arms, near the middle of the picture, parliament is in session. The flags and umbrellas indicate what the weather was like.

orable downpour. On that occasion, parliament elected Sveinn Björnsson to be the first, provisional, president of the republic, as there was no time to hold direct elections for the presidency. Since then, 17 June has been Iceland's national day.

Sveinn Björnsson was Iceland's first emissary to Copenhagen, in 1920–24 and 1926–41. He was Viceroy of Iceland 1941–44, and then President until his death in 1952.

29 Postwar Politics

IN THE AUTUMN OF 1944, THE Independence, Labour and Socialist parties formed a coalition headed by Ólafur Thors, leader of the Independence Party. This administration, calling itself the Innovation Government, set out to modernise the trawler fleet and construct a social security system second to none in other countries. The Cold War put an end to the Innovation Government in 1947, as will be discussed in the following chapter, but the formation of this coalition signalled permanent consensus between the two main branches of politics, right and left, on economic policy. Both sides were in agreement that the government should nurture business, both private and state enterprise, since much of the trawler fleet was operated by local authorities.

Consensus was reached that Iceland should aim to become a welfare state on the Scandinavian model.

Politics in the period 1947–59 were typified by unstable coalition governments. In the spirit of the Cold War, attempts were made to create a coalition of the self-styled democratic parties, i.e. Labour, Progressive and Independence. In 1950 the Labour Party found itself in opposition, along with the Socialist Party, and the right-wing Independence and Progressive parties attempted to govern together. In 1956 the Progressive Party switched over to form a left-wing government with the Labour Party and the newly-founded People's Alliance (Chapter 27). This government resigned in 1958, mainly due to disagreement on means of stabilising prices and

In parliament, 63 members sit in a unicameral assembly, elected from six constituencies.

wages. The economy had been the principal concern of governments in this period. The national deficit was counteracted by rationing and import controls. Inflation was combated by regulations on maximum retail margin and price levels, together with constant opposition to the unions' demands for higher pay. In comparison with later periods, inflation was not high at this time, averaging 10% per year, but it is impossible to say what it might have been without anti-inflationary measures.

In 1959–71, the Independence and Labour parties remained continuously in office together in an administration called the Restoration Government. This abolished import controls and strove to introduce a free market system. The government's primary concern was still inflation, which rose to an average of 12%. The last years of the period were difficult, as the herring catch failed and the price of cod dropped in the USA. This, together with the government's mishandling of the dispute over fishing limits (Chapter 31), meant that they lost their majority in the election of 1971.

After 1971 another series of unstable coalitions followed, and lasted for two decades, until the Independence Party regained the leadership, to keep it for another two decades in coalition with various parties. During the earlier period, inflation spiralled out of control, averaging 35% per year, and peaking in 1983 at 86%. But in 1990 the union movement agreed to severe cuts in wage levels in order to escape the vicious circle of rising wages and prices. After that inflation remained

–GÆTI VERIÐ ÍSLENSK KRÓNA

Inflation meant that the exchange rate of the Icelandic króna was constantly falling, and this is the subject of Gísli J. Ástþórsson's cartoon. In 1981 a new króna was introduced, worth 100 times more than the old króna. "Could be an Icelandic króna", the person says after observing the object under the microscope.

within reasonable limits for almost two decades. Had the Icelanders finally learned to maintain a stable economic system?

30 Cold War

When the Americans took on the defence of Iceland in 1941 (Chapter 28), an undertaking was given that they would leave as soon as the hostilities ceased. But by the time World War II came to an end in 1945, their policy had changed, and they wished to retain military facilities in Iceland permanently. The Icelanders refused this request, but the Americans made no move to go; and in fact it was arguable that the war had not formally ended until a peace treaty had been concluded. In the autumn of 1946 Ólafur Thors, prime minister and minister of foreign affairs, finally reached an agreement with the USA regarding facilities at the Keflavík air base for civilian staff, in connection with military transports to and from Europe. This agreement was approved by parliament, but only by 32 votes to 19. The entire Socialist Party and some Labour and Progressive party members felt the agreement was an unacceptable violation of Iceland's policy of neutrality. At this point the Socialists broke up the Innovation coalition (Chapter 29), and the Cold War took over Icelandic politics.

The following years clearly demonstrated American interest in Iceland. US Marshall Aid (1948–52) was intended to help Europe recover from the war, and the Icelanders, should logically have contributed to such aid rather than receiving it (Chapter 28). But in the event they received almost twice as much per head from Marshall Aid as any other European nation. During this period, the policy of neutrality was also abandoned. In 1949 Iceland became one of the founding

Crowds dispersed by tear gas on Austurvöllur, Reykjavík, 30 March 1949. Freeze-frames from a film of the incident.

nations of NATO on the condition, not recorded in any treaty document, that no military forces should be stationed in Iceland in times of peace. Iceland's membership was approved by parliament on 30 March, by 37 votes again 13. Outside Parliament House, the public cast their votes by throwing rocks, until the police dispersed the crowds using tear gas.

In spite of undertakings to the contrary, the USA secretly asked in 1951 for permission to bring troops

The US military strove to gain popularity in Iceland, for instance by inviting visits to the base. A group of Icelanders are seen here visiting the Keflavík air base. At the front are women in Icelandic national costume, one of the strongest symbols of Icelandic national consciousness.

to Iceland. The government called a secret meeting of members of parliament of all parties except the Socialist Party, in order to gain their consent. According to the government, all agreed to the treaty on a military base.

About 5,000 American troops were brought to Iceland, most of them to the Keflavík air base. For a long time the military provided employment for some one to two thousand Icelanders, and revenue from the military normally amounted to about 5% of foreign currency earnings.

The US military presence was for many years the most conten-tious issue in Icelandic politics. The Socialist Party and its successor, the People's Alliance, always demanded the resumption of neutrality, and the departure of the military. The Independence Party was equally resolute in its support for NATO membership and US defence. The Progressive and Labour parties generally supported NATO membership, but the left-wing government formed by them with the People's Alliance in 1956 made the departure of the military a policy issue. This demand was withdrawn, however, after the Soviet invasion of Hungary in 1956. After the end of the Cold War, around 1990, the Americans gradually lost interest in stationing a military force in Iceland. The Icelandic government tried unsuccessfully to induce them to stay on. The base at Keflavík Airport was abandoned in September 2006. Once again Iceland is a country without armed forces.

The flag of the United States is taken down as the Icelandic one is hoisted at Keflavík Airport on 30 September 2006.

31 Sovereignty at Sea

WHEN THE ICELANDERS GRADUALLY took over the protection of their territorial waters in the interwar years, 1918–39, fishing limits extended three nautical miles (5,556 metres) from the coast. In bays, the three-mile line was drawn from the point where the bay was 10 nautical miles across. But shortly after World War II, when foreign vessels resumed fishing off Iceland, and the Icelanders were building up a new fishing fleet, an urgent need was perceived for wider powers of jurisdiction. At around that time, the US government set an example for a new policy; in 1945 it was declared that the continental shelf of the USA was under US jurisdiction, without defining the extent of the continental shelf further.

In 1948 Alþingi passed an Act on the Scientific Protection of Fishing Grounds on the Continental Shelf, which authorised the minister of fisheries to fix by regulation the extent of fishing limits. On the basis of the legislation, Iceland's fishing limits were gradually extended to 200 nautical miles in the period 1950–75. No international laws applied to the extent of national fishing limits at that time, and foreigners who fished off Iceland regarded all these unilateral extensions as illegal.

In 1950–52 the fishing limits were extended to four miles, now measured from the mouth of bays and fjords. British fishing-vessel operators answered by placing an embargo on the landing of Icelandic fish in Britain; the Icelanders, however, dealt with the embargo by winning new markets in the USA and Russia. Icelandic fishing limits were next extended, to twelve nautical miles, in 1958. British naval vessels were dispatched to the fishing grounds to guard British trawlers, and thus began what the British press called a Cod War. Both parties strove to avoid causing casualties, and the war consisted largely of threat and counter-threat. At this point a left-wing government was in power in Iceland (Chapter 29). Socialist Lúðvík Jósepsson signed the regulation on the extension of the

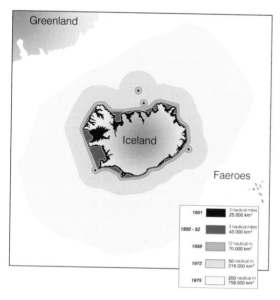

Greenland

Iceland

Faeroes

1901		3 nautical miles 25.000 km²
1950 - 52		3 nautical miles 43.000 km²
1958		12 nautical m. 70.000 km²
1972		50 nautical m. 216.000 km²
1975		200 nautical m. 758.000 km²

Extensions of fishing limits 1950–75. When the extension to 200 nautical miles was made, lines were drawn halfway between Iceland and its neighbouring countries – Greenland in the west and the Faroes in the east.

During the Cod Wars, collisions sometimes occurred between Icelandic coastguard ships and British naval vessels, and each generally blamed the other. British frigate after a collision with Icelandic coastguard vessel Týr.

fishing limits, and this caused considerable unrest in NATO ranks. When the Restoration Government of Independence and Labour parties came to power the following year, it was under great pressure to settle with Britain. This was achieved in 1961, when Britain recognised the twelve-mile fishing limit, and Iceland undertook to submit any further extensions of the fishing limit to the International Court in the Hague.

After the defeat of the Restoration Government in 1971, Lúðvík Jósepsson was again minister of fisheries. The following year the fishing limits were extended to 50 nautical miles. Britain responded with another Cod War, which ended a year later with a two-year truce.

Before this time had expired, the Independence Party had resumed leadership on this issue. In 1974 the party took over the fisheries ministry, and the following year fishing limits were extended to 200 miles. The Cod War resumed, and diplomatic relations between Britain and Iceland were broken off. But in the summer of 1976, a final agreement was reached. Britain retained limited fishing rights within

the 200-mile limit for six months. The Icelanders' campaign for independence in their fishing grounds ended with unequivocal victory.

Yet this did not solve all the problems. At this time, it transpired that the fish stocks off Iceland could not even sustain fishing by Iceland's own fleet. Shortly after this, fish quotas were allocated to vessel operators, on the basis of their prior fishing. This system is controversial, but no government has yet sought to marketise fishing rights.

Lúðvík Jósepsson, a socialist and a member of the People's Alliance, was minister of fisheries when fishing limits were extended in 1958 and in 1972. Abroad he was suspected of exploiting the fisheries dispute to undermine Iceland's relations with NATO, but he was probably motivated only by the interests of Iceland's fishing communities.

32 Liberated Women

LIKE OTHER WESTERN COUNTRIES, Iceland experienced a wave of radical re-assessment of conventional values around 1970. Young people experimented with communal living. Protest actions were common. Marginalised social groups made themselves heard; in 1978 homosexuals of both sexes formed, for instance, *Samtökin '78* ('78 Alliance).

Of these marginalised social groups, none was more vocal than women. Developments in women's rights in 1850–1923 (Chapter 24) had brought women mostly equal rights with men in formal terms, but in practical terms gender roles remained similar. Before 1970 very few women graduated from

Women's Day Off, 24 October 1975. Mass meeting in central Reykjavík.

university, while female members of parliament numbered one, two, or none. The Icelandic Women's Rights Association, however, remained active, campaigning principally for equal pay. Results were achieved in two stages, for public employees in 1945 and for unskilled employees in the private sector in 1961–67. But this legislation is generally regarded as being far from ensuring true equality of pay for equivalent work.

In 1970 women initiated a campaign for the re-examination of all conventional ideas of what women could do and what they deserved. A new movement was formed, the Red Stockings (*Rauðsokkahreyfingin*). The movement was too radical and provocative to gain a mass following, but

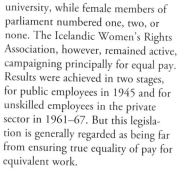

women who would never have attended a Red Stockings' meeting nonetheless applied the movement's methods. Thus on 24 October 1975 women took a mass day off from work, and even from their domestic tasks, in order to underline the importance of their contribution in society. In Reykjavík a rally on this day was attended by 20 to 25 thousand people, 20% of the population of the greater Reykjavík area.

Five years later a woman, Vigdís

Vigdís Finnbogadóttir, president of Iceland 1980–96, gave Icelandic women courage to play a more active role in politics.

until it joined the Social Democratic Alliance (Chapter 27). The Women's Alliance was never in government, and perhaps its greatest influence was in gradually opening up opportunities in other political parties to women. Now 38% of members of parliament are women (24 women, 39 men). In the present government, however, there are only four women, and six men. On the boards of financial institutions and firms, women are still rare. In that field equality has not yet been achieved. Nevertheless, the higher profile of women is probably the greatest change in Icelandic society in the last three decades of the 20th century.

Finnbogadóttir, was elected president of Iceland. We in Iceland maintain that she was the first woman democratically elected to the presidency of a nation. Vigdís was, admittedly, only successful because three male candidates opposed her, thus splitting the vote. But Vigdís won widespread popularity during her sixteen years as president, and was much admired both in Iceland and abroad.

Following the election of President Vigdís, many women felt it was time to enter the political arena. In 1982, women's lists stood in local elections in Reykjavík and Akureyri, and won two council seats in each.

For the general elections the following year, the Women's Alliance (*Samtök um kvennalista*) was formed, and stood for election in three constituencies, gaining 7.6% support in those constituencies, and three seats in parliament. The Women's Alliance continued to take part in elections, with parliamentary representation of three to six seats at each election,

One of the leading women in Icelandic politics around the turn of the century was Ingibjörg Sólrún Gísladóttir. In municipal elections in Reykjavík in 1994 she led a joint list of all opponents of the Independence Party, and won a majority after more than six decades of rule by the Independence Party. She was mayor of Reykjavík for nine years before becoming leader of the Social Democratic Alliance, and was a government minister 2007-09.

33 Expansion, Collapse of the Banks and Reconstruction

As mentioned above (Chapter 29), in the 1990s the Icelandic financial system began to function like that of any other capitalist society. A coalition government of Independence and Progressive Parties, headed by Independence Party leader Davíð Oddsson, came to power in the summer of 1995, and decided to pursue this development further. A large part of the economy was at that time still state-owned, including the two biggest banks, and various investment funds intended to finance different sectors of the economy. In 1997–98 these funds united to form an investment bank, which was privatised and in turn merged with another large private bank. During the early 2000s controlling shares in the state-owned banks were sold to groups of private investors. It later transpired that the purchase had been largely financed by loans from the other bank.

After the expansion period many new buildings stood unused, as they were not needed. Most were in Reykjavík, but not all. This seven-storey block of flats in the fishing village of Grindavík was inhabited by just one woman, at least from December 2007 to February 2009.

This marked the start of a huge expansion of the Icelandic economy. Financial institutions were able to borrow from abroad with extraordinary ease, and this led to a massive boom, mainly in construction of both residential and commercial buildings. It must have been obvious that construction was far outstripping demand, but individual contractors seem to have been confident that they would not be left with unsellable properties – although someone else might. Demand for labour soared, and workers flocked to Iceland, mostly from Poland.

This was followed by foreign investment. Icelandic banks and other corporations bought up companies abroad: a famous department store and an old luxury hotel in central Copenhagen, chains of fashion and food shops in Britain. The turnover of the Icelandic banks was soon many times more than Iceland's GDP. This was called "expansion," and people suggested that it was in the Icelandic character to acquire wealth abroad, like their Viking ancestors. In 2007 a young Icelander, Björgólfur Thor Björgólfsson, was reported to be the 249th wealthiest man in the world. All this collapsed in the recession which swept the world in 2008. In under three weeks in September and October all three major banks were declared insolvent and taken over by the state. A large proportion of Icelandic businesses were practically bankrupt. Many families were so heavily in debt that they appeared to have no hope of meeting their obligations.

Since then, the Icelanders have

In Britain and the Netherlands the Icelandic Landsbanki opened a deposit institution named Icesave, which attracted huge deposits. When the bank collapsed British and Dutch authorities demanded that the Icelandic state participate in paying the depositors. This cartoon shows British Prime Minister Gordon Brown and Iceland's Finance Minister Steingrímur J. Sigfússon negotiating on the issue.

been trying to work their way out of recession. A government of the Independence Party and Social Democratic Alliance had been in office since 2007. The government was perceived as being slow to react to the crisis, and a growing protest movement demanded its resignation. Ultimately the government stood down, and a general election was held in April 2009. The Independence Party lost its position as Iceland's largest party, and the Social Democratic Alliance and Left-Green Movement formed a coalition government, with SDA leader Jóhanna Sigurðardóttir as Prime Minister. For an entire electoral

term, until 2013, that government strove to restore the Icelandic economy. Many hard decisions had to be made, but overall the government did what it had set out to do. Perhaps the situation had not been as dire as the media had maintained: Icelanders' lifestyles, at least, gave little indication of poverty or lack.

The electorate was strangely ungrateful to the Social Democratic Alliance for its leadership in addressing the crisis, as we shall see in the next chapter.

Prime Minister Jóhanna Sigurðardóttir had a colourful political career. She first took a seat in the Alþingi for the Labour Party in 1978. Later she ran for the leadership and was defeated, left the party, launched a new political group and represented it in the Alþingi, until she became one of the founders of the Social Democratic Alliance in 1999. Her words when she lost the leadership contest have been much quoted: "My time will come." And her time came indeed in 2009, when opinion polls showed that the public had more confidence in her than anyone else, to lead the nation out of the crisis.

Latest Update

THROUGHOUT THE 20TH CENTURY the fisheries were Iceland's major source of foreign currency earnings, but since 2010 tourism has overtaken the fisheries, and now yields more foreign currency revenue than any other sector of the economy. This does not reflect any decline in the value of fish exports. The rise in tourism is in part due to an international trend: people are travelling more than ever before. But events in Iceland also contributed to the trend. In April 2010 a volcanic eruption under the Eyjafjallajökull ice cap commenced with huge emissions of ash. Safety guidelines prohibited planes from flying through clouds of volcanic ash, and so aviation was halted for a time – not only between Iceland and other countries, but throughout most of Europe. Icelanders feared that this would have a disastrous impact on tourism, and to counteract the damage a publicity campaign was launched: *Inspired by Iceland*. It was such a huge success that

the number of tourists in Iceland rose by 20–40% yearly from 2011 to 2017.

Together with high prices for fish products on world markets, growing tourism has meant that the Icelandic economy has flourished, incomes have risen, unemployment is minimal, and the Central Bank of Iceland has accumulated foreign currency reserves. Inflation practically disappeared. The exchange rate of the Icelandic *króna* (ISK) has risen so high that it may even pose a threat to the economy by making Iceland less competitive internationally.

In the political arena, these have been eventful years. As discussed in chapter 27 above, from 1938 to 1999 four parties dominated Icelandic politics, often in more-or-less unchanging proportions. Since 2000 new parties have increasingly won substantial support in parliamentary elections. In 2007 and 2009 new political groups won only about 10% of votes in total, while in 2013 they accounted

The eruption of Eyjafjallajökull in 2010 led to an unforeseen explosion in tourism to Iceland, which looks set to continue indefinitely.

In 2016 a new president of Iceland was elected. The people chose historian Guðni Th. Jóhannesson (right), seen here taking over office from his predecessor, President Ólafur Ragnar Grímsson, who had been in office for 20 years, longer than any other president.

for 25%, 38% in 2016 and 35% in 2017. At the same time, support for the four old-established parties has fluctuated more than in the past. The Progressive Party doubled its support in 2013, and in 2016 and 2017 it lost all that it had gained. The Social Democratic Alliance declined from nearly 30% support in 2009 to 5.7% in 2016 and 12.1% in 2017. The Independence Party and the Left-Green Movement have not yet experienced such setbacks, but in the present situation anything can happen.

The common factor of the new political groups is mainly that they challenge left-right divisions in politics. In general they campaign for freedom and human rights. To a historian in his seventies, they may seem a little unclear on policy, even immature. But they mean well. Groups that have campaigned on a platform of extreme nationalism and xenophobia have, on the contrary, gained little support.

In parliamentary elections in 2017, four groups from outside the main four parties were elected to parliament. The Centre Party (10.9%, 7 seats) was a newcomer on the scene founded by former Progressive Party leader. The People´s Party (6.9%, 4 seats) fights for better conditions for the poor and disabled. The Pirate Party (9.2%, 6 seats) is part of an international movement which is active in various countries, but only in Iceland has it gained substantial support. Restoration (6.7%, 4 seats) comprises largely former Independence Party supporters who, unlike the Independence Party, are in favour of Iceland joining the European Union.

At the time of writing, the Independence Party has formed a government with the Left-Green Movement and the Progressive Party. And that is the latest news from Iceland for the time being.

	1999	2003	2007	2009	2013	2016	2017
Independence Party	40,7	33,7	36,6	23,7	26,7	29,0	25,2
Progressive Party	18,4	17,7	11,7	14,8	24,4	11,5	10,7
Social Democratic Alliance	26,8	31,0	26,8	29,8	12,9	5,7	12,1
Left-Green Movement	9,1	8,8	14,3	21,7	10,9	15,9	16,9
Bright Future					8,2	7,2	1,2
Pirate Party					5,1	14,5	9,2
Restoration						10,5	6,7
Centre							10,9
People's Party							6,9
Other	5,0	8,4	10,6	10,0	12,0	5,7	0,2

Support for Icelandic parties in parliamentary elections 1999–2017. Icelanders appear to have decisively turned their backs on being lifelong supporters of a certain party, as for a football club. Some people suggest that this means the end of the era of political parties.

List of Illustrations

37 Skúli Magnússon. Photo Rafn Hafnfjörð.
38 Rasmus Christian Rask. From Tímarit hins íslenzka bókmenntafélags IX (1888), opposite p. 1.
38 Jónas Hallgrímsson. From Fjölnir I.
39 Þingvellir by W.G. Collingwood. British Museum.
40 Jón Sigurðsson. National Museum, Mms. 3312. Photo E. Lange.
41 National Convention of 1851. Painting by Gunnlaugur Blöndal. © Estate of the artist/MYNDSTEF 2000. Owner Alþingi. Photo Kristján Pétur Guðnason.
41 King Christian IX. Photo Rafn Hafnfjörð.
42 Sheep. Photo Sigurður Sigmundsson.
43 Farm. Drawing by Dosso in Labonne: L'Islande. From Árni Björnsson and Halldór J. Jónsson: Gamlar þjóðlífsmyndir, nr. 34.
43 Family. Drawing by J. Ross Browne in The Land of Thor. From Árni Björnsson and Halldór J. Jónsson: Gamlar þjóðlífsmyndir, nr. 44.
44 Icelanders in Sarnia. Drawing in the Canadian Illustrated News, 13.11.1875. From Guðjón Arngrímsson: Nýja Ísland, p. 127.
45 Log cabin in New Iceland. The Manitoba Archives, New Iceland Coll. 340. From Guðjón Arngrímsson: Nýja Ísland, p. 176.
46 Market town. From Gunnar Karlsson: Frelsisbarátta Suður–Þingeyinga, opposite p. 337.
47 Schooners in Reykjavík harbour. National Museum, SEy 489. Photo Sigfús Eymundsson.
48 Alþingishúsið. From Árni Björnsson and Halldór J. Jónsson: Gamlar þjóðlífsmyndir, nr. 86.
49 1st December 1918. National Museum, ÓM/MÓL 27. Photo Ólafur Magnússon.
49 Hannes Hafstein. National Museum, TRG 137.1.
50 Bríet Bjarnhéðinsdóttir. National Museum, Mms. 21484. Photo Sigfús Eymundsson.
51 Women's celebration. Ljósmyndasafn Reykjavíkur. Photo Magnús Ólafsson.
51 Ingibjörg H. Bjarnason. National Museum, Mms. 21412. Photo Ólafur Magnússon.
52 The boat Stanley. Drawing by Sigurður Guðjónsson. From Gullkistan, endurminningar Árna Gíslasonar, p. 199.
53 The trawler Coot. Drawing by Bjarni Sæmundsson. From Heimir Þorleifsson: Saga íslenzkrar togaraútgerðar, opposite p. 96.
53 Trawler captains' homes. From Heimir Þorleifsson: Saga íslenzkrar togaraútgerðar, between pp. 120 and 121.
54 Miðbær in Seyðisfjörður. Sögusafn verkalýðshreyfingarinnar, from the collection of Sigurður Guttormsson, MFA.
55 Protest march. Ljósmyndasafn Reykjavíkur. Photographer unknown.
55 Jónína Jónatansdóttir. National Museum, Mms. 18615.
57 Jónas Jónsson of Hrifla. National Museum, Mms. 19180. Photo Jón Kaldal.
57 Seamen's Day 1938. Ljósmyndasafn Reykjavíkur. Photo Skafti Guðjónsson.
58 Sandbag fortifications. Ljósmyndasafn Reykjavíkur. Photographer unknown.
59 Founding of the republic. Photo Ámundi Hjörleifsson. From Lýðveldishátíðin 1944, p. 174.
59 Sveinn Björnsson. Photo Walter B. Lane. Life Magazine © Times Corporation. From Tómas Þór Tómasson: Heimsstyrjaldarárin á Íslandi 1939–1945.
60 The parliament. Morgunblaðið. Photo Þorkell Þorkelsson.
61 Cartoon by Gísli J. Ástþórsson. From Steinar J. Lúðvíksson: Hvað gerðist á Íslandi 1981.

62 Riots on Austurvöllur. From a film by Sveinn Björnsson. From Baldur Guðlaugsson and Páll Heiðar Jónsson: 30. marz 1949, between pp. 128 and 129.
63 On Keflavík Air Base. From the library of Efling.
63 Change of flags at Keflavík Airport 2006. Photo Vilhelm Gunnarsson.
65 British frigate. Photo Óli Tynes. From Sveinn Sæmundsson: Guðmundur skipherra Kjærnested II, p. 91.
65 Lúðvík Jósepsson. National Museum.
66 Women's Day Off. Photo Kristján Pétur Guðnason.
67 Vigdís Finnbogadóttir. Morgunblaðið.
67 Ingibjörg Sólrún Gísladóttir. Morgunblaðið. Photo Árni Sæberg.
68 Seven-storey block of flats in Grindavík. Photo Ragnar Axelsson.
69 Cartoon of Gordon Brown and Steingrímur J. Sigfússon. Gunnar Karlsson cartoonist.
69 Jóhanna Sigurðardóttir. Photo Alþingi.
70 Eyjafjallajökull. Photo: Jóhann Ágúst Hansen.
71 Ólafur Ragnar Grímsson and Guðni Th. Jóhannesson. Photo: Gunnar Geir Vigfússon.

Index

A few books about Iceland

Agnar Kl. Jónsson, *Stjórnarráð Íslands 1904–1964* I–II. Reykjavík, Sögufélag, 1969.

Agnes S. Arnórsdóttir, *Property and Virginity. The Christianization of Marriage in Medieval Iceland 1200–1600.* Århus, Aarhus University Press, 2010.

Almenningsfræðsla á Íslandi 1880-2007 I-II. Ritstjóri Loftur Guttormsson, Reykjavík, Háskólaútgáfan, 2008.

Anna Sigurðardóttir, *Vinna kvenna á Íslandi í 1100 ár.* Reykjavík, Kvennasögusafn Íslands, 1985.

Árni Björnsson, *Saga daganna.* [2. útg., aukin og endurbætt.] Reykjavík, Mál og menning, 2000.

Ártöl og áfangar í sögu íslenskra kvenna. Ritstjórar Erla Hulda Halldórsdóttir og Guðrún Dís Jónatansdóttir. Ný og endurbætt útgáfa. Reykjavík, Kvennasögusafn Íslands, 1998.

Ásgeir Blöndal Magnússon, *Íslensk orðsifjabók.* Reykjavík, Orðabók Háskólans, 1989.

Birgir Hermannsson, *Understanding Nationalism. Studies in Icelandic Nationalism, 1800–2000.* Stockholm Studies in Politics 110. Stockholm, Department of Political Science, 2005.

Björn Th. Björnsson, *Íslenzk myndlist á 19. og 20. öld.* Drög að sögulegu yfirliti I–II. Reykjavík, Helgafell, 1964–73.

Björn Þorsteinsson, *Island.* Under medvirken af Bergsteinn Jónsson og Helgi Skúli Kjartansson. Oversat af Preben Meulengracht Sørensen. København, Politikens forlag, 1985.

Björn Þorsteinsson og Bergsteinn Jónsson, *Íslandssaga til okkar daga.* Reykjavík, Sögufélag, 1991.

Boyer, Régis, *L'Islande Médiévale.* Paris, Société d'édition Les Belles Lettres, 2001.

Bragi Guðmundsson og Gunnar Karlsson, *Uppruni nútímans. Kennslubók í Íslandssögu eftir 1830.* Reykjavík, Mál og menning, 1988.

Byock, Jesse, *Island i sagatiden. Samfund, magt og fejde.* Oversat af Jon Høyer. København, C.A. Reitzels Forlag, 1999.

Byock, Jesse, *Viking Age Iceland.* London Penguin, 2001.

Debes, Hans Jacob, *Island – land og ríki.* Tórshavn, Føroya Skúlabókagrunnur, 1994.

Eggert Þór Bernharðsson, *Saga Reykjavíkur 1940–1990. Borgin* I–II. Reykjavík, Iðunn, 1998.

Einar Laxness, *Íslandssaga, Alfræði Vöku-Helgafells* I–III. Reykjavík, Vaka-Helgafell, 1995.

Gísli Jónsson, *Konur og kosningar. Þættir úr sögu íslenskrar kvenréttindabaráttu.* Reykjavík, Bókaútgáfa Menningarsjóðs, 1977.

Griffiths, John C., *Modern Iceland.* London, Pall Mall Press, 1969.

Guðjón Friðriksson, *Saga Reykjavíkur. Bærinn vaknar. 1870–1940* I–II. Reykjavík, Iðunn, 1991–94.

Guðmundur Hálfdanarson, *The A-Z of Iceland. The A to Z Guide Series, No. 229.* Lanham, Scarecrow Press, 2010.

Guðni Th. Jóhannesson, *The History of Iceland.* Santa Barbara, Greenwood, 2013.

Gullfoss. Mødet mellem dansk og islandsk kultur i 1900-tallet. Redigeret af Auður Hauksdóttir, Guðmundur Jónsson og Erik Skyum-Nielsen. København, Vandkunsten, 2015.

Gunnar Karlsson, *Ástarsaga Íslendinga að fornu. Um 870–1300.* Reykjavík, Mál og menning, 2013.

Gunnar Karlsson, *Handbók í íslenskri miðaldasögu* I–III. Reykjavík, Háskólaútgáfan, 2007–16.
  I: *Inngangur að miðöldum* 2007.
  II: *Landnám Íslands* 2016.
  III: *Lífsbjörg Íslendinga frá 10. öld til 16. aldar* 2009.

Gunnar Karlsson, *Iceland's 1100 Years. The History of a Marginal Society.* London, Hurst & Company, 2000. – Same book: *The History of Iceland.* Minneapolis, University of Minnesota Press, 2000.

Gunnar Karlsson og sagnfræðinemar Háskóla Íslands, *Samband við miðaldir. Námsbók í íslenskri miðaldasögu, um 870–1550, og sagnfræðilegum aðferðum.* Reykjavík, Mál og menning, 1989.

Gustafsson, Harald, *Mellan kung och allmoge – ämbetsmän, beslutsprocess och inflytande på 1700-talets Island. Acta Universitatis Stockholmiensis* 33. Stockholm, Almqvist & Wiksell, 1985.

Hagskinna. Sögulegar hagtölur um Ísland. Icelandic Historical Statistics. Ritstjórar / Editors Guðmundur Jónsson, Magnús S. Magnússon. Reykjavík, Hagstofa Íslands, 1997.

Hallgerður Gísladóttir, *Íslensk matarhefð.* Reykjavík, Mál og menning, 1999.

Hastrup, Kirsten, *Culture and History in Medieval Iceland. An anthropological analysis of structure and change.* Oxford, Clarendon Press, 1985.

Helgi Skúli Kjartansson, *Ísland á 20. öld*.
Reykjavík, Sögufélag, 2002.

Ísland í aldanna rás. Saga lands og þjóðar ár frá ári [1700– 2010]. Sex bindi.
Aðalhöfundar Illugi Jökulsson, Bjarki Bjarnason, Björn Þór Sigbjörnsson, Bergsteinn Sigurðsson. Reykjavík, JPV útgáfa, 2003–10.

Íslandssagan í máli og myndum. Ritstjórar Árni Daníel Júlíusson og Jón Ólafur Ísberg. Reykjavík, Mál og menning, 2005.

Íslensk bókmenntasaga I–V. Reykjavík, Mál og menning, 1993–2006.

Íslensk þjóðmenning I, V–VII. Reykjavík, Þjóðsaga 1887–90.

Íslenskur söguatlas I–III. Ritstjórar Árni Daníel Júlíusson, Jón Ólafur Ísberg, Helgi Skúli Kjartansson. Reykjavík, Almenna bókafélagið / Iðunn, 1989–93.

Jón R. Hjálmarsson, *Die Geschichte Islands. Von der Besiedlung zur Gegenwart*. Reykjavík, Iceland Review, 1994.

Jón R. Hjálmarsson, *History of Iceland. From the Settlement to the Present Day*. Reykjavík, Iceland Review, 1993.

Jón R. Hjálmarsson, *Islands historie. Fra bosættelsen til vore dage*. Reykjavík, Iceland Review, 1999.

Jón R. Hjálmarsson, *Ístoría na Íslandíja. Ot zaselvaneto do nashí dní*. [S.l.], Riva, 2007.

Jón Jóhannesson, *A History of the Icelandic Commonwealth. Íslendinga saga*. Translated by Haraldur Bessason. Winnipeg, University of Manitoba Press, 1974.

Jón Jóhannesson, *Islands historie i mellomalderen. Fristatstida*. Oversatt av Hallvard Magerøy. Oslo, Universitetsforlaget,1969.

Jón Viðar Sigurðsson, *Chieftains and Power in the Icelandic Commonwealth*. Translated by Jean Lundskær-Nielsen. Odense, Odense University Press, 1999.

Kadecová, Helena, *Dejiny Islandu*. New York, NLN, 2001.

Kristni á Íslandi I–IV. Ritstjóri Hjalti Hugason. Reykjavík, Alþingi, 2000.

Kuhn, Hans, *Das alte Island*. Düsseldorf, Eugen Diederichs Verlag, 1971.

Lacy, Terry G., *Ring of Seasons. Iceland, its Culture and History*. Text and Photos. Reykjavík, University of Iceland Press, 1998.

Lúðvík Kristjánsson, *Íslenzkir sjávarhættir* I–V. Reykjavík, Bókaútgáfa Menningarsjóðs, 1980–86.

McTurk, Rory (ed.), *A Companion to Old Norse-Icelandic Literature and Culture*. Oxford, Blackwell, 2005.

Miller, William Ian, *Bloodtaking and Peacemaking. Feud, law, and society in saga Iceland*. Chicago, University of Chicago Press, 1990.

Orri Vésteinsson, *The Christianization of Iceland. Priests, Power, and Social Change 1000–1300*. Oxford, Oxford University Press, 2000.

Rosenblad, Esbjörn, & Sigurðardóttir-Rosenblad, *Iceland from Past to Present*. Translated by Alan Crozier. Reykjavík, Mál og menning, 1993.

Rosenblad, Esbjörn, *Island i saga och nutid*. Stockholm, Norsteds Förlag, 1990.

Rosenblad, Esbjörn, & Sigurðardóttir-Rosenblad, *Island von der Vergangenheit zur Gegenwart*. Übersetzt von Gudrun M.H. Kloes. Reykjavík, Mál og menning, 1999.

Saga Alþingis I–V. Reykjavík, Alþingis-sögunefnd, 1956.

Saga Íslands. Samin að tilhlutan Þjóðhátíðarnefndar 1974. Ritstjóri Sigurður Líndal. I.–XI. Reykjavík, Hið íslenska bókmenntafélag, 1974–2016.

Silfur hafsins, gull Íslands. Síldarsaga Íslendinga I–III. Reykjavík, Nesútgáfan, 2007.

Stjórnarráð Íslands 1964–2004 I–III. Ritstjóri Sumarliði R. Ísleifsson. Reykjavík, Sögufélag, 2004.

Sverrir Jakobsson, *Auðnaróðal. Baráttan um Ísland 1096–1281*. Reykjavík, Sögufélag, 2016.

Uppbrot hugmyndakerfis. Endurmótun íslenskrar utanríkisstefnu 1991–2007. Ritstjóri Valur Ingimundarson. Reykjavík, Hið íslenska bókmenntafélag, 2008.

Valur Ingimundarson, *Í eldlínu kalda stríðsins. Samskipti Íslands og Bandaríkjanna 1945–1960*. Reykjavík, Vaka-Helgafell, 1996.

Valur Ingimundarson, *Uppgjör við umheiminn. Samskipti Íslands, Bandaríkjanna og NATO 1960–1974. Íslensk þjóðernishyggja, vestrænt samstarf og landhelgisdeilan*. Reykjavík, Vaka-Helgafell, 2001.

Þóra Kristjánsdóttir *Mynd á þili. Íslenskir myndlistarmenn á 16., 17. og 18. öld*. Reykjavík, JPV útgáfa, 2005.